This book belongs to:

Christmas 2000

Christmas
with Southern Living
2000

Oxmoor
House

Christmas
with Southern Living
2000

Edited by Rebecca Brennan,
Julie Gunter, and Lauren Brooks

CONTENTS

ISBN: 0-8487-1959-X
ISSN: 0747-7791
Printed in the United States of America
Second Printing 2000

Editor-in-Chief: Nancy Fitzpatrick Wyatt
Senior Editor, Copy and Homes: Olivia Kindig Wells
Senior Foods Editor: Susan Payne Stabler
Art Director: James Boone

Christmas with Southern Living 2000

Editor: Rebecca Brennan
Foods Editor: Julie Gunter
Assistant Editor: Lauren Caswell Brooks
Copy Editor: Cathy Ritter Scholl
Editorial Assistant: Suzanne Powell
Associate Art Director: Cynthia R. Cooper
Designer: Emily Albright Parrish
Senior Photographers: Jim Bathie, John O'Hagan
Senior Photo Stylist: Kay E. Clarke
Photo Stylist: Linda Baltzell Wright
Stylist Assistants: Cathy Harris, Cathy Mathews
Illustrator: Kelly Davis
Director, Test Kitchens: Elizabeth Tyler Luckett
Assistant Director, Test Kitchens: Julie Christopher
Recipe Editor: Gayle Hays Sadler
Test Kitchens Staff: Rebecca Mohr Boggan;
    Gretchen Feldtman, R. D.; Natalie E. King; Jan A. Smith
Contributing Test Kitchens Staff: Kathleen Royal Phillips,
    Kate M. Wheeler, R. D.
Publishing Systems Administrator: Rick Tucker
Director, Production and Distribution: Phillip Lee
Books Production Manager: Larry Hunter
Production Assistant: Faye Porter Bonner

TIDINGS OF JOY

*Special events are the order of the day during this
season of the year. Grand-scale decorating,
a holiday workshop, and a family's Christmas feast
are the highlights of this chapter.*

JOYFUL HARMONY

This stately home's holiday trimmings are scaled to perfection.

Decorating a large home for Christmas can be challenging. How do you fill rooms with the cozy, familiar accoutrements of the holidays while matching the family favorites to the scale of the house? For this historic Southern home, the owners used some tried-and-true techniques to create Christmas decorations that are harmoniously proportioned to the house, something to be considered for any size home.

▶ In the entry hall, sparkling gold decorations and white twinkle lights give all who enter a cheery first impression. The Christmas tree in the far corner of the hall is a strong focal point and is just the right size to anchor the smaller vignettes in the entry. The side table showcases a papier-mâché nativity scene, which is lovingly unpacked and displayed year after year. Creamy white poinsettias and grapevine trees wrapped with tiny fairylike lights fill the space beside the staircase. Framing the setting is a fluffy green garland, embellished with lights and golden bows, trailing along the banister.

Fresh evergreen garlands, sweeping from window to window and over the door, and large wreaths above the door and side windows offer a traditional welcome in keeping with the style of the house. A bundle of greenery and a crisp, red bow trim the lamppost.

8

▲ A large oval table in the center of the entry hall provides ample space to feature the fresh fruits and flowers of the season. A bountiful assortment of green pears and vases of roses and lilies fills the home with wonderful aromas. Gold grapevine angels and tall ivy topiaries add luxuriant texture and necessary height to the tabletop arrangement. Lengths of gold fabric and ribbons wind around the bowls and vases, enhancing the enchanted forestlike ambience.

▶ Clippings from the yard supply all the materials needed to embellish the mantel in the library. Moist florist foam in a waterproof container forms the base for the arrangement and keeps the greenery fresh. The free-form display of privet, elaeagnus, holly, magnolia, hemlock, leucothoe, and nandina berries is a classic accent against the limestone fireplace and in keeping with the dark paneling of the room.

A moss-package centerpiece has become a family tradition on the breakfast room table. Small boxes are covered with sheet moss and tied with ribbon. Seeded eucalyptus is tucked in the bow for a finishing touch. Around the boxes are brightly colored ornaments and candles shaped as ornaments. (For a larger, outdoor version of this decoration, see page 35.)

TRIMMING THE TREE It takes a total of six days to assemble and decorate the tree each year. More than ten thousand lights are used, and all of the decorations are wired to the branches.

Of all the decorations, it's the 25' Christmas tree that is the true family favorite. The first year this oversize tree was placed in the tall-ceilinged conservatory, it posed a bit of a decorating dilemma. Ordinary-size ornaments were lost on the tree, and it would take forever to fill the branches.

Inspired by a similar tree at the Biltmore House in Asheville, North Carolina, the family wrapped large boxes to resemble Christmas gifts and wired the boxes to the tree to hold them in place. It took about two days to wrap approximately four hundred boxes with shiny wrapping paper and to wire them to the branches of the tree. (The boxes can be reused, thank goodness!) The glossy paper reflects the tree's white lights and casts a magnificent glow around the tree. Large gold cherubs and toy French horns fill in around the packages.

THE SOUTHERN FEAST

Christmas dinner in the South is all about relishing uninterrupted family time around the table. May this feast—complete with loving tabletop touches and a foolproof plan—inspire you to experience the day to the fullest.

Menu for 8
Roast Turkey with Thyme Butter and Shallots • Last-Minute Gravy
Rustic Corn Dressing • Apple Salad • Walnut Cranberry Sauce
Roasted and Smashed Sweet Potatoes • Gratin of Broccoli in Béchamel
Shredded Brussels Sprouts
Cheesecake Flan • Deep-Dish Pecan Pie

Planning Timetable

1 TO 2 WEEKS AHEAD:

•Check supply of chairs, serving dishes, flatware, and glassware. Arrange to borrow if necessary.
•Make out grocery list. Shop for nonperishables.

2 TO 3 DAYS AHEAD:

•Get out china, serving dishes, and utensils. Polish silver.
•Shop for perishables.
•Place frozen turkey in refrigerator to thaw.
•Prepare and freeze flavored ice cream, if desired.

1 DAY AHEAD:

•Plan centerpiece. Buy flowers or clip and gather winter berries and branches from your garden. Make place cards.
•Chill beverages. Make extra ice.
•Prepare and bake Cheesecake Flan and Deep-Dish Pecan Pie. Cover and chill.
•Prepare Walnut Cranberry Sauce. Cover and chill.
•Chop ingredients for Rustic Corn Dressing. Cover and chill.
•Prepare Roasted and Smashed Sweet Potatoes according to make-ahead directions. Cover and chill.

CHRISTMAS MORNING:

•Set table.
•Prepare Apple Salad. Cut fresh broccoli into spears. Slice brussels sprouts. Cover and chill all.

3 TO 4 HOURS BEFORE THE MEAL:

•Roast turkey.
•Prepare dressing; do not bake. Cover and chill.

1 HOUR BEFORE THE MEAL:

•Bake dressing.
•Prepare Gratin of Broccoli in Béchamel. Do not broil.
•Reheat Roasted and Smashed Sweet Potatoes.
•Prepare Shredded Brussels Sprouts.

JUST BEFORE SERVING:

•Prepare gravy.
•Broil Gratin of Broccoli in Béchamel.

BEFORE SERVING DESSERT:

•Brew coffee.
•Invert chilled flan onto a rimmed serving plate.
•Remove pie from springform pan; place on serving plate.

AT THE TABLE ▼

•Copper blends well with the colors of Christmas. And this menu displays a subtle copper scheme. Various serving pieces, the place cards, the chandelier decoration, and even the desserts carry the copper shade.

•It's fairly easy to add a theme or color scheme to your holiday table. Pull out your favorite serving pieces, old and new china, holiday place mats, candles, napkins, and napkin rings. Most likely there will be a common thread among your accoutrements; it might be a color, pattern, shape, or texture. Before you know it, you'll be mixing and matching elements for a beautifully original table.

A Place for Cards ▲

•Let place cards be a warm welcome to your holiday table. Show off the simplicity of fresh produce: Buy small Seckel pears and rub them with copper Rub 'n Buff paint. Then look for copper "T" garden labels or place cards at a garden shop (see Where to Find It, page 172) and write names on labels using a ballpoint pen. Insert the pointed ends of labels into painted pears. You can use the same tags to introduce recipes, as we did for the desserts in this menu.

Chandelier Can Do ▼

•Pressed for space on the table? Then transform your chandelier into a centerpiece, allowing your family and guests freedom for easy visiting across the table during the meal. (Or, if space permits, extend your arrangement from table-top to overhead, as we did.)
•We wrapped ribbon around the rims of antique copper cups and strung the cups to the chandelier. Then we added a splash of water to the cups and filled them with cut flowers, greenery, and seasonal berries. (Don't fill cups too full with water or flowers, or they may be too heavy to suspend safely from a chandelier.)

◀ Sipping Selections

•Pinot Noir is an all-purpose, affordable red wine. It's an excellent selection for this Christmas menu. A medium-bodied Chardonnay provides a popular white wine option that will complement roast turkey and all the trimmings. Serve Chardonnay well chilled and Pinot Noir lightly chilled or at room temperature.
•To choose a wine that pleases you, just read the back label of a wine bottle for a description of its particular characteristics.
•For the children, try serving Cranapple juice, apple juice, or sparkling Catawba.

◀ Keeping the Meal Hot

•Just minutes before the meal, fill or rinse serving dishes, platters, and gravy boat with very hot tap water; drain and dry. Fill with hot food and serve.

ROAST TURKEY WITH THYME BUTTER AND SHALLOTS

If you're diligent about basting this bird near the end of roasting, you'll end up with moist, golden results. Plump shallots nestled around the turkey get caramelized in the pan drippings as they roast, and make an easy decoration for the platter.

1 (14-pound) turkey
Salt and freshly ground pepper
¾ cup unsalted butter, softened
2 tablespoons chopped fresh thyme
12 large shallots
2 tablespoons olive oil
Garnish: fresh thyme sprigs

If you buy a frozen bird, remember to allow at least 3 days for it to thaw in the refrigerator.

Remove giblets and neck from turkey; reserve for making homemade broth, if desired. Rinse turkey with cold water; pat dry. Sprinkle cavity with salt and pepper. Place turkey, breast side up, in a greased broiler pan.

Combine softened butter and 2 tablespoons chopped thyme, stirring well. Using fingers, carefully loosen skin from turkey at neck area, working down to breast and thigh area. Spread ¼ cup butter mixture under skin.

Tie legs together with heavy string, or tuck them under flap of skin. Lift wingtips up and over back, and tuck under bird. Generously rub salt and pepper over turkey. Tent turkey loosely with aluminum foil; roast at 325° for 1 hour.

Melt remaining thyme butter in a small saucepan over low heat; set aside for basting.

Peel shallots and place in a bowl; drizzle with olive oil and sprinkle generously with salt and pepper. Set aside.

Uncover turkey; baste with several tablespoons melted thyme butter mixture. Roast 1 hour, basting occasionally with butter mixture. After second hour of roasting, scatter shallots in pan around turkey; baste turkey. Roast 1 more hour or until a meat thermometer inserted into meaty part of thigh registers 180°, basting turkey and shallots every 15 minutes with butter mixture and pan drippings.

When turkey is done, carefully transfer it to a serving platter; arrange shallots around turkey. Cover with foil, and let turkey rest 15 minutes before carving. Reserve drippings in pan for Last-Minute Gravy. Prepare gravy. Garnish platter just before serving, if desired. **Yield:** 14 servings.

LAST-MINUTE GRAVY

Don't clean your broiler pan before making gravy. That's where all the goodness is. We suggest whisking the gravy right in the same pan while the roasted turkey rests on a platter. We think you'll like the sweet tang apple cider adds to the recipe.

½ cup reserved pan drippings
½ cup all-purpose flour
1½ cups apple cider
1½ cups turkey or chicken broth
¾ teaspoon salt
¾ teaspoon freshly ground pepper

Set broiler pan over 2 burners. Whisk flour into drippings in pan. Cook over medium heat until flour mixture (roux) is dark golden, stirring constantly to loosen any browned bits from bottom of pan. Gradually add cider and broth; cook, stirring constantly, 5 to 10 minutes or until gravy is thickened. Stir in salt and pepper. **Yield:** 3 cups.

RUSTIC CORN DRESSING

Smoked bacon and roasted corn make this dressing unique.

1 (29-ounce) can whole kernel corn, drained (2¾ cups)
1 pound smoked bacon (we tested with Nueske's)
2 cups chopped onion
1½ cups chopped celery
4 cloves garlic, chopped
½ cup butter or margarine, melted
6 cups (12 ounces) stuffing (we tested with Pepperidge
   Farm cubed country-style stuffing)
1½ cups coarsely chopped pecans, toasted
1 large egg, lightly beaten
2 to 2¾ cups chicken or turkey broth
½ teaspoon salt
1 teaspoon freshly ground pepper

Press corn between several layers of paper towels to remove excess moisture. Set aside.

Cook bacon in a large skillet over medium heat until crisp; remove bacon, reserving 2 tablespoons drippings in skillet. Crumble bacon; set aside. Add corn to skillet; toss to coat. Cook over high heat, stirring constantly, until corn is roasted in appearance. Transfer to a large bowl.

Cook onion, celery, and garlic in butter in large skillet over medium-high heat, stirring constantly, until tender. Transfer to large bowl. Add stuffing, crumbled bacon, and pecans, stirring well. Add egg, desired amount of broth, salt, and pepper to stuffing mixture; stir gently.

Spoon dressing into a lightly greased 13" x 9" pan. Bake, uncovered, at 325° for 1 hour or until well browned. **Yield:** 10 servings.

APPLE SALAD

We recommend Fuji, Braeburn, Jonagold, or Gala apples for this simple salad. Give it time to chill before serving.

5 to 6 apples, chopped (8 cups)
4 stalks celery, chopped (2 cups)
1 cup coarsely chopped pecans
1 cup chopped pitted dates
1 cup mayonnaise
2 tablespoons sugar
2 tablespoons milk

Combine first 4 ingredients in a large bowl; toss well.

Combine mayonnaise, sugar, and milk, stirring until blended. Add mayonnaise mixture to apple mixture, tossing to coat. Cover and chill. **Yield:** 12 cups.

Take Your Pick

Although the big three apples–Red and Golden Delicious and Granny Smith–are always a hit, there are some spectacular new apple varieties cropping up in the marketplace. We recommend that you try any of the following firm, crisp apples in our holiday Apple Salad.

FUJI
•Flavor: Sweet with intense apple and pear notes.
•Uses: An excellent apple for baking and for eating out of hand or using in fresh salads.

BRAEBURN
•Flavor: Mildly sweet/tart with intense apple flavor and good aromatics.
•Uses: All-purpose apple for eating out of hand or using in savory dishes or desserts.

JONAGOLD
•Flavor: Moderately sweet/tart.
•Uses: Good choice for cooking and baking or using in fresh salads.

GALA
•Flavor: Sweet and aromatic.
•Uses: Best eaten out of hand or used in fresh salads or desserts.

WALNUT CRANBERRY SAUCE

A hint of cinnamon, splash of dark vinegar, and handful of toasted nuts make this cranberry sauce worthy of gift giving. Deliver it in a jar tied with ribbon.

1 (16-ounce) can whole-berry cranberry sauce
⅓ cup strawberry preserves
1½ tablespoons sugar
¼ teaspoon ground cinnamon
½ cup coarsely chopped walnuts, toasted
1 tablespoon balsamic vinegar or red wine such as Pinot Noir

Combine first 4 ingredients in a saucepan. Cook over medium heat, stirring often, just until thoroughly heated. Remove from heat; stir in walnuts and vinegar. Cover and chill until ready to serve. Serve with turkey or ham. **Yield:** 2¼ cups.

ROASTED AND SMASHED SWEET POTATOES

These sweet potatoes get caramelized during roasting, so when you mash them a wonderful rich and sweet flavor comes forth. A small dollop makes the perfect serving.

3 pounds sweet potatoes, peeled and cut into 1½" chunks
3 tablespoons olive oil
¾ teaspoon salt
½ teaspoon freshly ground pepper
¼ cup butter or margarine, cut into pieces
⅔ cup half-and-half, heated
¼ cup firmly packed light brown sugar

Place sweet potato chunks in a large greased roasting pan; drizzle with olive oil. Sprinkle with salt and pepper; toss well. Spread sweet potato chunks in a single layer. Roast at 400° for 30 to 40 minutes or until sweet potatoes are very tender and roasted in appearance, stirring occasionally.

Transfer roasted sweet potatoes to a large bowl while still warm; add butter and mash with a potato masher. Add half-and-half and brown sugar; mash until fluffy. Serve warm. **Yield:** 8 servings.

Make-Ahead: *Transfer roasted sweet potatoes to a Dutch oven or large saucepan; add butter and mash. Cover and chill overnight. Before serving, let sweet potato mixture stand at room temperature about 30 minutes. Add half-and-half and brown sugar; cook over low heat until thoroughly heated, mashing until fluffy.*

GRATIN OF BROCCOLI IN BÉCHAMEL

A gratin is simply a dish, savory or sweet, that's finished under a broiler to create a golden crust. Sometimes the crust comes from breadcrumbs; sometimes it's merely cheese, as in this delicious side dish bathed in béchamel sauce.

2½ pounds fresh broccoli, cut into spears
3 tablespoons butter or margarine
3 tablespoons all-purpose flour
2 cups milk
2 tablespoons stone-ground mustard
⅛ teaspoon salt
⅛ teaspoon freshly grated or ground nutmeg
⅛ teaspoon pepper
1 cup (4 ounces) shredded Gruyère cheese

Arrange broccoli in a steamer basket over boiling water. Cover and steam 10 minutes or just until tender. Remove from heat. Transfer broccoli to a lightly greased 2-quart gratin or other shallow baking dish.

Meanwhile, melt butter in a heavy saucepan over medium heat; add flour, stirring until smooth. Cook 1 minute, stirring constantly. Gradually add milk, stirring constantly. Cook, stirring constantly, until sauce is thickened and bubbly. Remove from heat; stir in mustard and next 3 ingredients. Pour sauce over broccoli; sprinkle with cheese. Broil 5½" from heat 6 to 8 minutes or until lightly browned. Serve hot. **Yield:** 8 servings.

SHREDDED BRUSSELS SPROUTS

This recipe will make anyone a fan of brussels sprouts. Clean and slice the brussels sprouts ahead and store them in a zip-top plastic bag. Then just heat your skillet for a fast stir-fry with great sweet 'n' tangy flavor.

2 pounds brussels sprouts
2 tablespoons butter or margarine
2 tablespoons olive oil
2 cloves garlic, minced
½ small purple onion, cut into slivers (½ cup)
½ teaspoon salt
½ teaspoon pepper
¼ cup plus 2 tablespoons red wine vinegar
1½ tablespoons brown sugar

Wash brussels sprouts; remove discolored leaves. Cut off stem ends and thinly slice brussels sprouts. (They should look shredded.)

Heat butter and oil in a large deep skillet or Dutch oven over medium-high heat until hot. Add shredded brussels sprouts, garlic, and onion slivers. Sauté 8 to 10 minutes or until brussels sprouts are tender and onion is lightly caramelized. Season with salt and pepper; transfer to a serving bowl. Add vinegar and brown sugar to skillet. Simmer over medium heat 30 seconds; pour over brussels sprouts, and toss gently. Serve hot. **Yield:** 8 servings.

CHEESECAKE FLAN

Savoring the contrast between this incredibly rich baked custard and its slightly burnt-tasting caramel sauce is a delicious experience.

¾ cup sugar
4 large eggs
3 slices white bread, crusts removed
1 (14-ounce) can sweetened condensed milk
1 (8-ounce) carton mascarpone cheese (1 cup)
1 cup evaporated milk
⅔ cup water
3 tablespoons butter or margarine, melted
1 teaspoon vanilla extract

Sprinkle sugar in a heavy skillet. Cook over medium heat, stirring constantly with a wooden spoon, until sugar melts and turns light brown. Remove from heat. Quickly pour hot caramel into a 9" round cakepan, tilting to coat bottom; set pan aside. (Caramel syrup will harden and crack.)

Combine eggs and remaining 7 ingredients in a large food processor or blender. Process just until smooth, stopping once to scrape down sides. Pour custard mixture over syrup in cakepan. Place cakepan in a large shallow pan. Cover cakepan with aluminum foil. Add hot water to shallow pan to depth of 1". Bake at 350° for 50 to 55 minutes or until knife inserted off center comes out clean. (Center should still be slightly liquid; flan will finish cooking as it cools.)

Remove cakepan from water bath; cool flan completely on a wire rack. Cover and chill several hours or overnight. Loosen edges of flan with a spatula, and invert flan onto a rimmed serving plate, letting caramel sauce drizzle over the top. **Yield:** 1 (9") flan.

Note: *We found that a large food processor worked best for blending this flan. Otherwise we recommend using a blender.*

Flan defined: Flan is the Spanish cousin of the French crème caramel. Made with sweetened condensed milk rather than milk or cream, flan is an egg-rich custard baked in a caramel-lined pan, unmolded and served in its own glassy caramel sauce.

Mascarpone defined: Pronounced (mas-kar-POHN), this intensely rich fresh cow's milk cheese comes from northern Italy. Find it in the gourmet cheese/deli section at large supermarkets.

Deep-Dish
Pecan Pie

Cheesecake
Flan

DEEP-DISH PECAN PIE

This is the grande dame of pecan pies. It slices best when chilled and served the next day. Make your servings small for this pecan-packed decadent dessert.

1 cup butter or margarine, softened
2 (3-ounce) packages cream cheese, softened
2 cups all-purpose flour
¼ cup sugar
1 (16-ounce) bottle light corn syrup (2 cups)
1½ cups firmly packed light brown sugar
⅓ cup butter or margarine, melted
4 large eggs, lightly beaten
4 egg yolks, lightly beaten
1 tablespoon vanilla extract
½ teaspoon salt
3½ cups pecan pieces or halves

Beat 1 cup butter and cream cheese at medium speed of an electric mixer until creamy. Gradually add flour and ¼ cup sugar, beating well. Shape dough into a flat disc; cover and chill 15 minutes. Roll chilled dough to a 13" circle; carefully transfer to an ungreased 9" springform pan. (We recommend covering the outside of your springform pan with aluminum foil before filling and baking this pie. It's a safeguard against leaks.) Press dough up sides of pan. Cover and chill.

Combine corn syrup, brown sugar, and melted butter in a large bowl; stir well with a wire whisk. Add eggs, egg yolks, vanilla, and salt; stir well. Stir in pecans. Pour filling into unbaked pastry-lined pan.

Bake at 375° for 15 minutes. Reduce oven temperature to 300°; bake 2 hours and 15 minutes, shielding pie with aluminum foil to prevent excess browning, if necessary. Cool completely on a wire rack. Cover and chill, if desired. Remove sides of springform pan to serve. **Yield:** 1 (9") pie.

Ice Cream Ideas

FLAVORED CREAM

If you're looking for a dollop of something to top the Deep-Dish Pecan Pie, stir up one of these fancy flavored ice creams. Freeze the cream several hours, or days, before your big holiday meal.

3 cups vanilla ice cream, softened
3 tablespoons Frangelico or Kahlúa, or ¼ cup spiced rum, or 1½ tablespoons instant espresso coffee granules

Place ice cream in a large bowl. Drizzle with desired liqueur or sprinkle with coffee granules; stir well. Spoon ice cream into individual storage containers, cover, and freeze until firm. To serve, spoon small dollops of ice cream onto pie. **Yield:** 3 cups.

Note: Ice cream stores easily in small amounts in disposable, rigid plastic containers available at large supermarkets.

Leftover Lagniappe

Lagniappe (lan-yap) means a little something extra. What more could you add to a sumptuous Christmas feast other than the thought of tasty leftovers? The only thing as good as the big meal itself may be what's left to nibble on the next day. These two delicious recipes make smart use of remaining turkey—if you can forego that tempting turkey sandwich.

Turkey Pot Pie

TURKEY POT PIES

1 cup chopped peeled red potato
1 cup chopped carrot
1 cup frozen baby lima beans
1 cup chopped onion
⅓ cup butter or margarine, melted
⅓ cup all-purpose flour
2 cups chicken broth
1 cup half-and-half
4 cups chopped cooked turkey
1½ tablespoons minced fresh sage
1 teaspoon salt
½ teaspoon pepper
1½ (17¼-ounce) packages frozen puff pastry, thawed
1 egg yolk, lightly beaten
1 tablespoon half-and-half

Cook potato and carrot in boiling water to cover 5 minutes. Add lima beans; cook 5 minutes or until crisp-tender. Drain vegetable mixture; set aside.

Cook onion in butter in a Dutch oven over medium heat, stirring constantly, until tender. Add flour; cook, stirring constantly, 1 minute. Add broth and 1 cup half-and-half; cook, stirring constantly, until mixture is thickened and bubbly. Stir in turkey and vegetable mixture. Stir in sage, salt, and pepper.

Spoon mixture into 4 (2-cup) ovenproof soup bowls.

Roll puff pastry to ⅛" thickness on a lightly floured surface. Cut circles of pastry large enough to cover tops of bowls (5" to 6"). Combine egg yolk and 1 tablespoon half-and-half; brush half of egg mixture onto edges of pastry circles. Invert over turkey mixture in each bowl. Fold edges under and crimp. Cut decorative shapes from remaining pastry, if desired, arranging cutouts in center of pies. Brush top of each pot pie with remaining egg mixture.

Bake at 400° for 15 to 20 minutes or until pot pies are golden. Serve hot. **Yield:** 4 servings.

CREAM OF TURKEY AND RICE SOUP

After you've feasted on your holiday bird, here's a delicious idea for the carcass.

1 turkey carcass
½ cup butter or margarine
½ cup all-purpose flour
1 large onion, chopped (about 1½ cups)
2 shallots, chopped
3 large carrots, scraped and chopped
3 stalks celery, sliced
1 cup uncooked long-grain rice
1½ teaspoons salt
½ teaspoon pepper
2 teaspoons chopped fresh thyme or ½ teaspoon dried thyme
1 cup whipping cream

Place turkey carcass in a large stockpot or Dutch oven; add water to cover. Bring to a boil; cover, reduce heat, and simmer 1 hour. Remove carcass from broth, reserving 10 cups broth. Cool carcass, and pick meat from bones. Set meat aside.

Melt butter in stockpot over medium-high heat. Add flour and cook 5 minutes, stirring constantly. (Roux will be a blond color.) Add onion, shallots, carrot, and celery to roux; reduce heat to medium. Cook 10 minutes, stirring often. Stir in reserved broth, turkey meat, rice, salt, pepper, and thyme; bring to a boil. Cover, reduce heat, and simmer 20 minutes or until rice is tender. Add whipping cream; simmer, uncovered, 5 minutes or to desired thickness. **Yield:** 3½ quarts.

A WORKSHOP THAT'S ALL PLAY

Learning is fun in this refined antiques shop setting where creating holiday tablescapes is the lesson of the day.

A bright Saturday morning in early November launched the holiday season for a lovely gathering of neighbors and friends eager to learn how to create lavish tablescapes from stylist Kay Clarke (far right). A cozy shop, Henhouse Antiques, provided a partylike setting for the session in decorating inspiration. Winter-blooming plants in an outdoor planter offered a fragrant greeting (below).

▶ **FRUIT AND FLOWERS** This bountiful tablescape spans the season from Thanksgiving to Christmas. Using a wooden barrel from the shop as a container, Kay started the centerpiece with a row of clementines (tiny tangerines) as the base and built up from there using holly, roses, seeded eucalyptus, and apples. Kumquats on bamboo skewers fill the center of the arrangement. Citrus pomanders studded with cloves and star anise fill a platter. The vivid contrast created with the blue bottles and blue-and-white china enhances the warm color scheme.

SHADES OF RED Several elements set this tablescape apart: Kay selected a white ironstone tureen as the container for the centerpiece; she combined shades of red that are not commonly considered complementary, strengthening the mono-chromatic color scheme; and she eschewed the idea that a centerpiece must be low on the table. As Kay says, "This is a buffet party look. It's festive and joyful and designed to be viewed from all angles."

28

Kay's Tips for Tablescapes

1. For a festive pomander, hot-glue star anise around the center of a piece of citrus. For the bow, wrap wire around the ribbon and push it into the fruit.

2. Fill small vases (the kind used for forcing bulbs into bloom) with fresh flowers and greenery. Tie them securely to the chandelier as an extension of the centerpiece, visually continuing the floral design upward from the table.

• When dining table space is at a premium, decorate just the chandelier in lieu of a centerpiece.

• Use long, untied lengths of ribbon in arrangements, when possible. Recycle the ribbon for different purposes.

3. Think beyond the centerpiece when creating a tablescape; consider the color and pattern of plates, glassware, and table and chair fabrics.

• Fill bowls with seasonal fruit and berries to add rich color and texture to the tabletop.

4. To make the container a highly visible part of the centerpiece, keep the materials tight around the container's top edge and build up from there.

• Slightly opened roses are often preferable to tight buds. To coax the blooms to open, clip the stems and place the roses in a bucket of warm water overnight.

5. Fruit "kabobs" are an easy way to add height to an arrangement. Bamboo skewers work perfectly for small fruit, such as these kumquats. For heavier fruit, use florist picks.

◀ ELEGANCE IN WHITE AND GREEN ▲

For this sideboard decoration, Kay arranged green arti-
chokes and pears, creamy white roses, and white snow
berries in an antique silver samovar. Seeded eucalyptus
pods enhance the silver tones of the container and the
mirror hanging above the sideboard. A variety of small
containers filled with flowers is placed on the silver tray
around the centerpiece, creating a more elaborate display.

▶ METALLIC ACCENTS

Small Seckel pears and diminutive kumquats are the key
ingredients in a glistening topiary and garland. Kay gave
the fruits metallic highlights with gold, silver, and copper
Rub 'n Buff. The kumquats are strung on a wire, and
ribbon bows are tied at intervals along the garland. For
the topiary, Kay attached the burnished pears to a
Styrofoam cone with florist picks and filled in with moss
and ribbons. Kay's advice: "Think about the parties and
get-togethers you have planned for the season, and use
materials that will last from one event to the next."

GREETING THE SEASON

*Feel the excitement of Christmas
in the air, and express that wonder in
spirited decorations for your home.*

OUTWARD CHARM

Your outdoor decorations share the warm, festive spirit of the season with every passerby. Whether you fancy fruit and greenery or big boxes wrapped in fluffy moss, these pages show many ways to put on a fresh face for the holidays.

◀ SIMPLY DIVINE

An ordinary rope spray-painted gold adds astonishing sophistication to a plain evergreen garland. Bold tassels are easily made by knotting the rope ends and unraveling the strands for an unexpected flourish. On the front door, pomegranates and pinecones add color and texture to a mixed greenery wreath. Use florist picks and wire to secure the fruit and pinecones to the wreath.

▲ BIG ON CHARM

These oversize packages are a fanciful way to show your enthusiasm for the season. Glue sheet moss to a large cardboard box, and tie the box with wide ribbon. For an accent, wire or hot-glue clusters of artificial fruit to the top of the box. Be sure to place the boxes under a covered entry to keep them looking their best.

FRESH TRADITIONS

▲ A large pineapple, the symbol of Southern hospitality, commands center stage in this opulent fanlight arrangement. To assemble, purchase a semicircular wooden form from a crafts or hardware store. Outline the form with magnolia leaves, nailing or stapling them to secure. Hammer nails through the back of the form, and push the pineapple and lemons onto the nails. Wire small bunches of boxwood sprigs together, and tack in place among the lemons.

◀ Place a Styrofoam or wire cone-shaped form in an outdoor planter. Attach clusters of aucuba leaves, lemons, and pears to the form with florist wire and picks. A fresh pineapple makes a grand topper.

▶ The fruit-laden front door tree uses a 1" sheet of Styrofoam as its base. After assembling the base (see the diagrams and directions on page 166), cover the tree with sheet moss, securing it with U-shaped florist pins. Pin or hot-glue artificial fruit and silk holly sprigs in alternate rows at an angle across the tree. For the trunk, cut in half a papier-mâché pot (available at crafts or floral-supply shops). Hot-glue the pot to the trunk (see page 166). Tuck moss into the top of the pot. For the hanger, punch two small holes at the top of the tree, thread a pipe cleaner through the holes, and twist it to form a loop. Top the tree with a fluffy bow.

SMOOTH TRANSITION

The vibrant look of this home's exterior decorations is repeated inside to awesome effect. Continuing the same colors and materials from the outside to the inside reinforces the strong scheme. The outdoor's crimson and gold tones are reflected in richly hued diamond-design ribbon on the indoor banister. Golden pears, grape clusters, berries, and bows are tucked into the greenery and held in place with florist wire. The entrance is made even more grand with the addition of small artificial trees "planted" in urns on the front porch and frosted with tiny white twinkle lights.

▶ STAMPED WITH STYLE

If your outdoor decorating time is limited, think of putting all your energy into an eye-catching mailbox arrangement. With just a bit of insider how-to, you'll find it's a surprisingly quick way to create a look that will stay fresh all season. For directions, see page 166.

▼ JINGLE BELL DOOR CHIME

Let the merry sounds of Christmas greet you each time you open the door. This little adornment is also fetching as a tree ornament or package topper. To make the chime, you'll need approximately 8 large jingle bells, narrow cording, and ribbon. If desired, wire a sprig of greenery and berries just under the bow. For diagrams and directions, see page 166.

▶ CANDLES IN THE SNOW

Grab a stack of galvanized buckets, and fill them with bright candles for cheery holiday luminarias. Ice cream salt poured in the buckets holds the candles in place and looks like mounds of frosty snow.

Climb the stairs to this home's festive entry and be met by a twinkling tableau of wee carolers and gaily wrapped packages. Strands of brilliant white lights float in the tall evergreen trees that flank the doors and the beribboned greenery garlands. Red bells top the garland's arch and adorn the handsome double doors.

◀ CUSTOMARY CLASS

Create the traditional symbol of greeting and goodwill with a wreath made from seasonal favorites—magnolia, holly, and hemlock. Add sparkle to the wreath by tucking ribbons among the greenery or by attaching glistening gold ornaments.

▲ CITRUS ACCENTS

This holiday start a new custom with a wreath made from uncommon materials. Aucuba leaves form the base with colorful accents provided by tangerines, limes, and lemons.

To make either of the wreaths shown here, cut plant materials into 6" to 8" pieces. Wire together small bundles that contain each kind of plant; then wire the bundles to a wire, straw, or vine wreath form, overlapping the bundles as you go. To attach a piece of fresh fruit to the wreath, pierce the fruit from side to side with a skewer; thread florist wire through the holes; and twist the wire around the wreath form to hold the fruit in place.

43

DECORATING DELIGHTS

The wreath is on the door, the outdoor lights are hung. Now it's time to dress your rooms in holiday finery.

ALL THAT GLITTERS

The rich luster of gold decorations is a handsome alternative to the season's customary reds and greens.

If reds and greens are not your thing, combine hints of gold with natural neutrals for holiday decorations that match any decorating scheme. Use an abundance of flowers, fruits, candles, nuts, berries, cones, branches, and ribbons—any materials you can find in luscious warm shades of gold to brown, ivory to peach. Let the ideas shown here and on the following pages inspire your decorations all through the house.

This table sets the gold standard in every detail, from the soft yellow gold of the pears to the caramel-colored turbinado sugar that fills the dessert dishes-cum-candleholders. Coppery ornaments and amber-hued glassware mix easily with white china plates and perky star candles for a sunny setting that fills the air with the magic of Christmas. The centerpiece has an antique cake stand as its base. A plate placed on top of the stand holds an assortment of small containers filled with flowers, striped candy, and candles. A florist foam wreath encircling the cake stand overflows with flowers and berries. To make the wreath, first soak the form in water, then trim the flower stems, and push the plants into the foam. Place the wreath on a plate to protect the tabletop, and water every few days to keep the flowers fresh.

Fresh flower wreaths are tied to the chair backs with sheer wired ribbon. After dinner, they can be left in place or moved to a window or door.

To make the wreath, soak a florist foam wreath in water. Cut the stems of your choice of fresh flowers, greenery, and berries, and push the plants into the foam. Continue until you achieve the desired fullness.

To keep the wreath fresh, every few days place it on a plate and gently pour water on it. Allow the water to drain from the wreath before putting it back in place. For a wreath that will stay fresh all season long, consider using silk flowers and greenery instead of fresh—or a combination of the two.

◀Natural materials such as long stems of curly willow, berries, pinecones, pears, and walnuts fill this mantel. A gold compote, piled high with burnished ornaments; shiny wine goblets; and candles add sparkling highlights. Handfuls of walnuts are perfect anchors for pillar candles in glass hurricane globes.

▼This table setting is a fine example of how different styles of china can mix together harmoniously. Notice that each of the plates is slightly different yet shares a complementary color scheme with the others.

When it's time for dinner, move the dessert dish candle-holder sitting on top of the plates to the side, where it can still cast a cozy glow over the table. Turbinado sugar, which has the consistency of sand, fills the dessert dish. Brown sugar can be substituted for the turbinado sugar, but it doesn't pour as easily and may become sticky.

To complete the setting, add a gracious place favor that doubles as a napkin holder. The aluminum cone filled with lollipops can be taken home and hung on the tree as a charming reminder of a special event.

GARLANDS OF GOLD
This sumptuous garland is the essence of understated elegance, yet it has such grand appeal it may be the star of your holiday show.

▲RITZY WREATH For the wreath, make the garland as described below, then shape it into the desired form and wire the ends together. This wreath has a rectangular shape but could easily be formed into a circle. For a circular wreath, wrap the garland around a wire wreath form to help maintain its shape. Because of the weight of the fruit, the rectangular wreath best maintains its shape when placed on a surface instead of being hung.

MAKING THE GARLAND

To form the garland, stagger the stems of gold holly and the fruit pieces, and wire or tape them together with brown florist tape. (All materials are available at crafts and discount stores.) Continue until you have the desired length of garland. A 7' garland uses approximately 8 large stems of holly and of fruit. (The holly stems used for the garland shown here have several branches coming from the main stem.)

To fill out the garland, wire on your choice of berry clusters, ornaments, and assorted embellishments. Add bows along the length of the garland or to the wreath, as desired.

GOOD SCENTS

Lovely to look at and even better to smell. That's what you'll find
with these fragrant ideas that use citrus, apples, and spices in fresh new ways.

CITRUS POTPOURRI BOWLS ▲

These dried fruit containers will last for a couple of months. To make the bowls, cut off the top of an orange, lime, lemon, or tangerine. Scrape out all of the fruit and as much flesh as possible from both sections; rinse the sections with cool water and let them dry.

To dry the sections, you can either dehydrate them in a food dehydrator; bake them in an oven at 125° for 8 to 12 hours, turning occasionally on the rack; or air-dry them in a warm, sunny place.

Once they are dry, fill the citrus bowls with potpourri, replace tops, and tie shut with raffia or ribbon. Accent with bay leaves, cinnamon sticks, or star anise, if desired.

◄ FRUIT AND SPICE SWAG

Though perfectly suited for the kitchen, this aromatic swag fills the air with wonderful scents anywhere you hang it. The basic materials are all artificial or dried, so you'll be able to use it year after year.

The swag shown here uses a 3' artificial garland, but you can vary the length, if desired. Cut two lengths of wire slightly longer than the garland. On one length, thread dried apple slices and on the other, thread dried orange slices. For each length of wire, secure one end of the wire to the end of the garland. Wind the wire along the length of the garland, spacing the fruit slices in a pleasing arrangement. Secure the wire ends at the end of the garland. Thread star anise onto shorter lengths of wire and attach to the swag at random intervals. Fill in with small fruit picks and fresh greenery, as desired.

DRIED APPLE CHAIR SWAG ▲

For a casual chair decoration, thread dried apple slices (available at crafts and discount stores) on a thin wire. The swag shown here uses a short length of wire for a simple drop, but you can form the wire into a wreath or use a longer length and drape it across the back of the chair. Wire nandina berries, sprigs of greenery, and cinnamon sticks at the top. Hide the wire with a bow.

BERRY CHRISTMAS

Bright red berries are natural ornaments. Here and on the next pages, we feature these tiny treasures in some appealing holiday decorations.

BERRY AND VINE TREES ▲

Nestle shiny sprays of berries among the branches of small grapevine trees for a quick, versatile, and festive display on the breakfast table, dining room sideboard, or living room mantel. You may find it helpful to trim some of the berries into shorter pieces and use wire to secure them to the tree. (Berry sprays and grapevine trees are available at crafts and discount stores.)

Here, the trees are surrounded by a coordinating Berry Garland, which can also be used to dress up a window (see photo, right) or wrap around the Christmas tree.

BERRY GARLAND ▶

To make the garland, stagger the stems of red berry sprays, and wire or tape them together with brown florist tape. For a 7' garland, we used approximately 10 stems of berry sprays. A spray has several thin branches with berries coming from one main stem. (All materials are available at crafts and discount stores.) Continue until you have the desired length of garland.

54

BERRY MANTEL ACCENTS

Cheery red candles and berries set a bright mood on this mantel. Branches of berries stand tall in urns that frame the setting, while the delicate raspberry wreath adds interest at the center of the arrangement.

To make the raspberry wreath, cover a wreath form with sheet moss. The wreath shown here is approximately 9". Hot-glue a variety of artificial or dried berries to the wreath. For the hanger, loop a ribbon around the wreath, and add a bow in front, if desired.

BERRY HIGHLIGHTS Berry sprays and greenery sprigs are carefully wired to a dining room chandelier, filling the room with the seasonal scent of cedar. We suggest using artificial or dried berries for a longer lasting display. Sheer gold ribbon tied into a bow around alternate lights adds a glowing warmth to the natural arrangement.

BERRY-FRESH CANDLE COLLARS

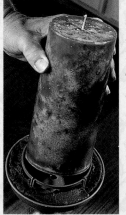

This candle trim can be used for tall candleholders that stand on the floor or for shorter ones that you would use on a mantel or tabletop. The technique is the same, but you'll want to adjust the scale of the materials to suit the setting.

To assemble the greenery candle collar, we used a candle adapter filled with florist foam that fits into the candleholder. Candle adapters are available at floral-supply stores. Precut rounds of florist foam, which are available at crafts and discount stores, can be substituted for the candle adapter. If you use florist foam, tape it crosswise with florist tape to the top of the candleholder to firmly secure. Soak the foam in water before you begin. Push sprigs of greenery and berries into the foam, using florist picks, if necessary. Use a florist pick in the bottom of the candle to secure it to the foam base, and make sure that the candle is tall enough so the flame never meets the greenery.

57

FIREPLACE FINERY

*Gather the family around the fireplace, and bask in the glow of the
spirited decorations you've created with inspiration from these pages.*

Instead of the usual wreath, this year make a bold literal statement of your love for the season. Fashion holiday letters from plywood cut into the shape of each letter. Top the wood with florist foam that has been soaked in water. Wrap chicken wire around the foam and the wood base to hold the foam in place. Cover the foam with greenery clippings. (Misting the greenery every few days will help keep it fresh.)

For letters you can use year after year, cut each letter from a sheet of Styrofoam. Cover the Styrofoam with sheet moss; then push sprigs of silk greenery and berries into the form. For a hanger, make a large loop from cording, and secure the ends on the back side of the letter.

The mantel scarf shown here is made from five napkins placed on top of the mantel. The tassels are held in place with double-faced mounting tape.

Fill your fireplace with the sparkle of dozens of candles. For the best arrangement, choose pillars in varying heights, along with some votives. Place some candles on bricks, and use clear glass candleholders or plates underneath the others. Fill in with greenery around the candles, being careful to avoid the flames. For safety, be sure to open the flue.

▲ Who says you have to put a tack in your mantel to display Christmas stockings? Make them a key part of your overall decoration instead. Here, the stockings take their place in a symmetrical arrangement composed of simple items that come together for a cozy, yet artful, look. (Here's a tip: Keep the stockings upright by stuffing them with bubble wrap or crumpled newspaper.)

◄ The mantel is a wonderful spot to display photographs from Christmases past, establishing a visual holiday history that everyone will enjoy. The gold and cranberry colors of the garland, stockings, and angel are a rich complement to the assorted frames. Note how nestling the stockings into the garland at the corners of the mantel treats them as an important part of the entire design.

▶ This is an excellent example of coordinating the mantel decoration with the room's existing decor. The dominant color of the grass cloth-covered walls is enhanced by the claret red-and-gold ribbon that is a feature of the garland-laden chimneypiece. Tiny gold berries and white twinkle lights contribute to the garland's opulent appearance.

The downy white flowers of baby's breath give this garland the look of fluffy snow. Ivory tapers in glass candleholders heighten the monochromatic effect. To make the garland, wire small bunches of baby's breath together with florist wire, staggering the bunches as you work. For a 7' garland, we used 5 large bundles of baby's breath. The amount of flowers needed will depend on the length of the garland and the size of the bundles. Wire big bows made from sheer ribbon to the garland, if desired.

White accents on this mantel convey the feeling of a bright winter morning. White pillar candles and sheer white ribbon are in crisp contrast to the deep richness of the evergreen garland. To keep the flowers on the garland fresh, place each stem in a plastic water vial (available at floral-supply and crafts stores), and hide the vials in the greenery.

NATURAL CHARM

The lowly pinecone is elevated to sophisticated new heights with light touches of paint and ribbon.

▲WOODLAND SWAG

Acorns and pinecones are natural complements in this beautifully elegant decoration. Shown here on a chair back, the festoon can also grace a mantel, window, or cupboard shelf. The number of pinecones and acorns you need depends on the length of your garland.

To string the pieces together, insert a large safety pin through an acorn, ¼" from the top. Using a large darning needle and plastic thread, push the needle through the hole in the acorn and then wrap the thread around the top of an inverted pinecone under the first layer of "petals." Continue in this manner, alternating acorns and pinecones, until you reach the desired length. Tie a thread loop at each end of the garland to use as a hanger.

▶SNOW-TIPPED PINECONES

Stack these large pinecones in a decorative container, and your holiday centerpiece is complete. Spray large pinecones with gold paint. When pinecones are dry, use a foam brush and a dabbing motion to apply joint compound (available at hardware, discount, and home-supply stores) to the outer edges of the pinecones. Allow the compound to dry completely before arranging.

▼ FROSTED PINECONE ORNAMENT

This frothy bauble looks ready to take flight with its sheer ribbon "wings." Spray-paint the pinecone with white paint, and hot-glue dainty berries and lightweight ribbon to the top of the inverted cone. Tie or glue a thin, satin ribbon to the top to use as a hanger. Thread assorted beads on a thin wire, and attach to the point of the ornament, concealing the wire ends in the pinecone.

▼ DOOR DECOR

This refined swag is right at home hanging from a pretty doorknob, but you'll find it also fits in nicely hanging above the mantel or on the wall. Spray the pinecones with gold paint, and apply joint compound to the outer edges as for the Snow-Tipped Pinecones. For the hanger, attach a big bow to each end of a length of ribbon. Attach one bow to the top of each pinecone with wire or hot glue.

KISSING BALLS

*Move over mistletoe—roses, greenery, and ribbon
bring variation to this Christmas tradition.*

ROSE KISSING BALLS For a romantic table setting, hang rose kissing balls at varying lengths from your chandelier. Clip the rose just below the bloom, leaving a small piece of stem. Gently push the stems into a Styrofoam ball. For extra stability, use a low-temperature glue gun to anchor the roses to the ball. Using U-shaped florist pins, pin ribbon to the top of the ball to make a hanger. Use different-colored roses for variety, if desired. Make these aromatic kissing balls the day of your event, and mist them with water to maintain their freshness.

GREENERY KISSING BALL

For an all-natural look, make this greenery ball using clippings from your yard. Cut sprigs of boxwood, holly, cedar, evergreen, and other greenery for a fresh, full look. Insert stems in a round oasis-in-cage base that has been soaked in water. The water will keep the ball moist and looking fresh for days. For the hanger, attach a ribbon loop to the top of the ball with a U-shaped florist pin.

RIBBON KISSING BALL

This shimmering kissing ball can be used year after year. Cut wired ribbon in 3" strips and fold in half to create loops. Attach the raw edges of the ribbon to a Styrofoam ball using straight pins. For extra fullness, cut the ends of several 3" strips of ribbon into V shapes and pin the opposite ends to the ball in a random fashion. For the hanger, attach a ribbon loop to the top of the ball with a U-shaped florist pin.

BOXWOOD KISSING BALL

Use boxwood clippings to create a simple, casual kissing ball. Wire small bunches of greenery together with wired florist picks, and push them into a Styrofoam ball, continuing until the ball is completely covered. Tie a multilooped bow with festive ribbon, leaving long tails. Pin the bow to the top of the ball, and trail the tails down the sides. For the hanger, attach a ribbon loop to the top of the ball with a U-shaped florist pin. To add a whimsical touch, attach a fanciful ornament to the ball with wire.

SET THE TABLE WITH FELT

*For an unexpected change of pace from traditional table coverings,
try these two ideas that are as fun to make as they are to use.*

◀ SNOWFLAKE TABLE RUNNER

For the table runner shown here, we used 3 yards of ivory felt, 3 yards of crimson felt, and 1 yard of paper-backed fusible web. The amounts you need may vary depending on the size of your table runner.

Measure the length of your table and add 16" to this length (for two 8" drops). Cut both pieces of felt to this length. Cut the ivory felt 30" wide and cut the crimson felt 16" wide.

Using the snowflake patterns on page 167, trace numerous snowflakes onto paper-backed fusible web. Cut out the snowflakes, leaving a ½" edge around the design.

Arrange the fusible-web snowflakes randomly on the wrong side of the crimson felt and fuse them in place. Cut out the snowflake design. Remove the paper backing.

Center the wrong side of the crimson felt against the right side of the ivory felt. Cover the snowflake "openings" with a press cloth and fuse in place on the ivory felt. Leave the outer edges unfused to give the appearance of two separate runners. Spot cleaning is recommended.

STARRY NIGHT PLACE MATS ▲

A 12" x 18" piece of precut felt called "Stiffened Eazy Felt" gets this project off to a quick start. The felt is available at crafts stores. You will need 2 rectangular pieces of felt for each place mat: one color for the background and another for the foreground. You will also need a 12" x 18" piece of paper-backed fusible web for each place mat.

On the paper side of the fusible web, mark 6" up from the bottom along one short side and 2" up from the bottom on the opposite side. Using a pencil, draw a sloping line from one side of the fusible web to the other, beginning and ending at the marks you just made. Using the tree and star patterns on page 167, trace 3 trees (onto the paper) along the slope; trace stars in the sky, as desired. Fuse the web to the wrong side of the foreground felt.

Cut along the slope line. Trim 1" away from the straight bottom edge of the lower section of felt. Cut out the trees and stars following the traced lines.

Remove the paper backing from the foreground felt and position the top section of the felt on top of the background felt. Adjust and/or trim the straight edges of the foreground felt so that approximately ⅛" of the background felt shows around the edges. Cover the top section of the foreground felt with a press cloth, and fuse to the background.

Remove the backing from the lower section of the foreground felt, and position it on top of the background felt so approximately 1" of the "slope" shows between the top and bottom of the foreground felt. Cover the lower section with a press cloth; fuse into place. Spot cleaning is recommended.

GATHERINGS

*Being with friends and loved ones is the best part of
the holidays. Here are some ideas for adding sparkle
and goodwill to all your seasonal get-togethers.*

OPEN HOUSE HORS D'OEUVRES

*Hosting a holiday open house?
It can be easy when you plan your
menu and prepare the food in advance.*

On these pages we offer a host of meaty appetizers, several dips and spreads, some spirited beverages, and a pair of desserts. Mix and match recipes from our listing below or explore one of our two menu ideas—a wine and cheese party with light fare (shown at right) or a hearty, more substantial menu (shown on page 80). Each serves 15 to 20 guests.

SANDWICHES
Smoked Salmon Canapés
Cheddar and Hot Mustard Sandwiches
Ham and Cranberry Cream Cheese Sandwiches
Mini Pork Sandwiches

FINGER FOOD
Black Bean Tartlets
Chicken Fingers with Apple Butter-Peanut Sauce
Roasted Red Pepper Bruschetta
Venison Meatballs in Dried Cherry Sauce

PASTRIES
Fig and Gruyère Palmiers
Curried Chicken Turnovers

DIPS AND SPREADS
Chunky Gorgonzola Dip
Sherried Mushroom Spread
Eggplant and Walnut Dip
Butternut Squash Spread on Cheese Croutons

BEVERAGES
Mulled Black Cherry Wine
White Hot Chocolate
Spiced Hot Buttered Rum Punch

DESSERTS
Lemon Fondue
Caramel-Almond Tartlets

Chunky
Gorgonzola Dip

WINE & CHEESE PARTY
menu for 15 to 20

- Smoked Salmon Canapés
- Fig and Gruyère Palmiers
- Chunky Gorgonzola Dip, sliced fruit, walnuts, crackers, breadsticks
- Cheddar and Hot Mustard Sandwiches
- Assorted cheeses for tasting

Note: *See individual recipes for wine recommendations.*

Fig and Gruyère
Palmiers

Cheddar and
Hot Mustard
Sandwiches

Smoked Salmon
Canapés

WINE & CHEESE CHAT

- We offer a wine recommendation for each recipe in this menu. Encourage your guests to sip small glasses of the various wines with each of the recipes. Or you may find that you want to offer just one or two wines that best fit the entire menu.
- All the recipes highlight cheese, but for added fun, consider incorporating a simple cheese tasting into your menu. Here are some basic guidelines:
- Pick high-quality cheeses.
- Do some sampling at your local cheese shop to help narrow the choices.
- Serve small samples of each cheese and encourage guests to eat slowly. A ½- to 1-ounce serving of each cheese is ample.
- A basic combination for a five-cheese tasting is: an aged Cheddar, a semisoft cheese like Camembert, an aged Swiss like Gruyère, a goat cheese, and a blue cheese.
- Above all, choose cheeses you like.

SMOKED SALMON CANAPÉS

Pair these upscale open-faced sandwiches with Pinot Noir. It complements salmon well.

½ (8-ounce) package cream cheese, softened
¼ cup sour cream
1 tablespoon honey
½ teaspoon freshly ground pepper
¼ teaspoon salt
24 slices party rye or pumpernickel bread
12 ounces smoked salmon
48 very thin slices cucumber
Minced purple onion
Freshly ground pepper
Garnish: fresh dill, separated into tiny sprigs

Combine first 5 ingredients in a bowl; beat at low speed of an electric mixer until thoroughly blended. Cut each bread slice diagonally in half. Separate salmon into very thin slices (smoked salmon should separate naturally into slivers). Cut salmon into 48 pieces.

Spread ½ teaspoon cream cheese mixture onto each piece of bread. Roll a cucumber slice inside each salmon piece; place over cream cheese spread on bread. Dollop ½ teaspoon cream cheese mixture over salmon. Sprinkle with onion and pepper; garnish, if desired. **Yield:** 4 dozen.

FIG AND GRUYÈRE PALMIERS

Fig preserves and Gruyère cheese taste great together in this easy French pastry called a palmier. *Be sure to line your baking sheets with parchment paper; it makes clean-up so easy. A light and slightly sweet Riesling or Gewürztraminer is our pick for these pastries.*

1 (17.3-ounce) package frozen puff pastry, thawed
2 cups (8 ounces) shredded Gruyère cheese
½ cup fig preserves, melted

Roll one puff pastry sheet into a 14" x 10" rectangle. Sprinkle with 1 cup Gruyère cheese. Roll each short side, jellyroll fashion, to meet in center. Repeat procedure with remaining puff pastry sheet and cheese.

Cut each roll into ¼" slices. Place slices on parchment paper-lined baking sheets; brush with melted preserves. Bake at 400° for 8 to 10 minutes or until golden. Serve warm. **Yield:** 56 appetizers.

Make-Ahead: You can make these pastries ahead and freeze the uncut, unbaked rolls. Wrap rolls in heavy-duty plastic wrap, and freeze. To serve, let rolls stand at room temperature 10 minutes before slicing. Brush with preserves and bake as above.

CHUNKY GORGONZOLA DIP

Gorgonzola is an aged, distinctively sharp blue-veined cheese that pairs naturally with fruit and walnuts. That's what we recommend you serve with this creamy dip, along with crackers and a spicy, steely Alsatian Gewürztraminer.

1 (8-ounce) carton mascarpone cheese (1 cup)
⅓ cup sour cream
⅓ cup chopped fresh chives
½ teaspoon salt
¼ teaspoon ground white pepper
4 ounces Gorgonzola cheese, crumbled (1 cup)
Garnish: chopped fresh chives

Combine mascarpone cheese and sour cream in a small bowl; stir with a wooden spoon until smooth. Stir in chives, salt, and pepper. Gently stir in Gorgonzola cheese, leaving dip chunky. Garnish, if desired. Serve dip with sliced apples and pears, crackers, and toasted walnuts. **Yield:** 2 cups.

CHEDDAR AND HOT MUSTARD SANDWICHES

Traditional English pub fare inspired the robust flavor of these simple sandwiches. Serve with ale or Merlot.

3 cups (12 ounces) shredded sharp Cheddar cheese
1 (4-ounce) jar hot mustard (we tested with Inglehoffer)
½ cup minced onion
¼ cup mayonnaise
12 slices pumpernickel bread, crusts removed (we tested with Pepperidge Farm)
12 slices sourdough bread, crusts removed (we tested with Cobblestone Mill)

Combine first 4 ingredients in a bowl; stir well. Spread about 3 tablespoons cheese mixture onto each pumpernickel bread slice. Top each with a sourdough bread slice. Cut each sandwich into four squares. Arrange sandwiches on a serving platter, some pumpernickel side up and some sourdough side up. **Yield:** 4 dozen.

Polka-Dot Sandwiches: To make sandwiches more artistic, cut 4 small circles from each pumpernickel slice and 4 small circles from each sourdough slice using a ¾" to 1" biscuit cutter. Place the white sourdough circles in the holes left in the pumpernickel slices; place the brown pumpernickel circles in the holes left in the sourdough slices. Assemble sandwiches as directed.

HAM AND CRANBERRY CREAM CHEESE SANDWICHES

Four ingredients become delicious holiday finger sandwiches with only a few minutes' work.

½ cup tub-style cream cheese, softened
½ cup whole-berry cranberry sauce
28 slices cinnamon-raisin bread, crusts removed (we tested with Pepperidge Farm)
28 very thin slices smoked ham (1¼ pounds)

Combine cream cheese and cranberry sauce, stirring well. Spread a heaping teaspoon cream cheese mixture onto each bread slice. Top half of bread slices with 2 slices ham. Place remaining bread, cream cheese side down, onto ham. Cut each sandwich into 4 triangles using a sharp knife. **Yield:** 56 appetizers.

SHERRIED MUSHROOM SPREAD

Sherry and tarragon team with earthy shiitake mushrooms in this luscious spread that's best on crisp crackers.

¼ cup unsalted butter
1 pound shiitake mushrooms, finely chopped (about 6 cups)
2 shallots, minced
¾ teaspoon salt
¼ teaspoon ground white pepper
2 tablespoons all-purpose flour
½ cup dry sherry
1 cup chicken broth
1 tablespoon chopped fresh tarragon or 1 teaspoon dried tarragon
¼ cup sour cream
Garnishes: thinly sliced green onion, chopped fresh tarragon, sliced shiitake mushroom

Melt butter in a large skillet over medium-high heat; add mushrooms and shallots. Sauté 6 to 7 minutes or until mushrooms release moisture. Sprinkle with salt and pepper; stir well. Sprinkle with flour, stirring to coat mushrooms; cook 1 minute. Add sherry, broth, and tarragon; simmer, uncovered, 10 to 15 minutes or until liquid is absorbed, stirring occasionally. Remove from heat; stir in sour cream.

Spoon mixture into a serving bowl. Garnish, if desired. Spread on melba toast rounds or crostini. **Yield:** 2⅓ cups.

BLACK BEAN TARTLETS

This Southwestern appetizer sports a red and green filling with spicy flavor.

1¼ cups all-purpose flour
¾ cup yellow cornmeal
½ cup (2 ounces) shredded Monterey Jack cheese with
    peppers
1 teaspoon salt
1 teaspoon ground cumin
1 teaspoon chili powder
½ teaspoon garlic powder
½ teaspoon ground red pepper
½ cup cold butter, cut into pieces
1 large egg, lightly beaten
2 tablespoons ice water
Black Bean Salsa
Garnishes: sour cream, fresh cilantro

Combine first 8 ingredients in a food processor; pulse until blended. Add butter; pulse until mixture is crumbly. Add egg and ice water; process just until the mixture forms a ball.

Divide dough in half; shape each half of dough into 16 (1") balls. Press balls into lightly greased miniature (1¾") muffin pans, pressing evenly into bottom and up sides.

Bake tartlet shells at 450° for 8 minutes or until lightly browned. Cool in pans 10 minutes; remove shells to wire racks, and cool completely.

Spoon 1 tablespoon Black Bean Salsa into each tartlet shell; garnish, if desired. Serve at room temperature. **Yield:** 32 appetizers.

BLACK BEAN SALSA

1 (15-ounce) can black beans, drained
2 canned chipotle chiles in adobo sauce, minced
3 green onions, chopped
½ cup finely chopped sweet yellow pepper
1 plum tomato, finely chopped
1 tablespoon chopped fresh cilantro
2 tablespoons fresh lime juice
1 tablespoon olive oil
½ teaspoon salt

Combine all ingredients in a bowl, tossing well. Cover and chill at least 1 hour. **Yield:** 2¼ cups.

Black Bean Tartlets

EGGPLANT AND WALNUT DIP

Mediterranean flavors prevail in this easy eggplant dip. Shop at an Asian market for the five-spice powder. It's the ingredient that gives this recipe a real depth of flavor.

2 small eggplants, cut in half lengthwise (about ¾ pound each)
1 cup chopped, toasted walnuts, divided
¾ teaspoon Chinese five-spice powder
½ teaspoon salt
2 tablespoons half-and-half
¼ cup plain low-fat yogurt
Garnishes: fresh chives, toasted walnuts

Place eggplant, cut sides down, in a well-greased 13" x 9" pan. Bake at 425° for 30 minutes or until very tender. Cool. Peel and coarsely chop eggplant. Place eggplant in a food processor; add ½ cup walnuts and next 4 ingredients. Process until smooth. Spoon eggplant mixture into a bowl, and stir in remaining ½ cup walnuts. Garnish, if desired. Serve with pumpernickel slices or pita bread. **Yield:** 2⅔ cups.

CHICKEN FINGERS WITH APPLE BUTTER-PEANUT SAUCE

The sauce for these chicken fingers is so good you'll want to dip into it again and again.

1 pound skinned and boned chicken breast halves
¼ cup all-purpose flour
1 teaspoon salt
½ teaspoon pepper
1 large egg, beaten
⅓ cup milk
½ cup Italian-seasoned breadcrumbs
¼ cup sesame seeds
¼ teaspoon salt
3 tablespoons butter or margarine, melted
Apple Butter-Peanut Sauce

Cut chicken into ¼" lengthwise strips. Combine flour, 1 teaspoon salt, and pepper in a large zip-top plastic bag. Add chicken strips, seal bag, and shake to coat.
Combine egg and milk in a shallow dish, stirring well. Combine breadcrumbs, sesame seeds, and ¼ teaspoon salt in a shallow dish. Dip chicken strips in egg mixture, and dredge in breadcrumb mixture. Place in a lightly greased 13" x 9" pan; drizzle with butter.

Cover and bake at 425° for 20 minutes; uncover and bake 18 to 20 more minutes or until done. Serve with Apple Butter-Peanut Sauce, using short wooden skewers. **Yield:** 10 appetizer servings.

APPLE BUTTER-PEANUT SAUCE

½ cup creamy peanut butter
⅓ cup apple butter
1¼ cups chicken broth
1 tablespoon freshly grated ginger
¼ teaspoon salt

Combine all ingredients in a small saucepan over medium-high heat. Bring just to a boil; reduce heat, and simmer, uncovered, 2 minutes or until thickened, stirring constantly. Remove from heat; cool. Serve at room temperature. **Yield:** 1¾ cups.

ROASTED RED PEPPER BRUSCHETTA

We topped these toasts with a sweet-tangy roasted red pepper mix and feta cheese. It's a pretty hors d'oeuvre for a holiday party. See it photographed on the next page.

1 (12-ounce) jar roasted red peppers, drained well and finely chopped
½ cup finely chopped plum tomato
¼ cup finely chopped purple onion
2 tablespoons balsamic vinegar
2 tablespoons olive oil
½ teaspoon salt
½ teaspoon freshly ground pepper
Dash of sugar
1 baguette, cut into 28 slices
¼ cup olive oil
Salt and pepper
½ cup crumbled garlic and herb-flavored feta cheese

Combine first 3 ingredients in a bowl. Combine vinegar, 2 tablespoons olive oil, salt, pepper, and sugar; pour over pepper mixture. Toss. Cover and chill until ready to serve.
Arrange baguette slices on a large ungreased baking sheet. Brush or drizzle slices with ¼ cup oil. Sprinkle with salt and pepper. Bake at 400° for 4 minutes or until barely toasted.
Spoon about 1 tablespoon pepper mixture onto each toast; top each with crumbled feta. Broil 5½" from heat 3 minutes or until bubbly and barely browned. Serve warm. **Yield:** 28 appetizers.

Butternut Squash
Spread on Cheese
Croutons

Roasted Red
Pepper
Bruschetta

BUTTERNUT SQUASH SPREAD ON CHEESE CROUTONS

Baked butternut squash and Asiago cheese blend with herbs and toasted pecans for a fabulous-tasting spread.

1 medium butternut squash
3 cloves garlic, minced
3 tablespoons butter or margarine, melted
½ (8-ounce) package cream cheese, softened
1½ cups freshly grated Asiago cheese, divided
1 tablespoon sugar
2 teaspoons chopped fresh thyme
2 teaspoons chopped fresh rosemary
½ cup chopped pecans, toasted
1 baguette, cut into 48 thin slices
½ cup olive oil
Salt and pepper
Garnishes: small sprigs of fresh thyme and rosemary

Cut squash in half lengthwise; remove and discard seeds. Place squash, cut side down, in a 13" x 9" baking dish. Add hot water to dish to depth of 1". Bake, uncovered, at 350° for 1 hour or until squash is tender.

Remove squash pulp, discarding shells. Mash pulp, and place in a large bowl.

Sauté garlic in butter in a small skillet over medium-high heat until golden. Add garlic to squash pulp in bowl. Add cream cheese, ½ cup Asiago cheese, and next 3 ingredients to bowl; mash until blended. Stir in pecans.

Place baguette slices on 2 large ungreased baking sheets; brush or drizzle olive oil over baguette slices. Sprinkle with salt and pepper. Bake at 400° for 4 minutes. Sprinkle baguette slices with remaining 1 cup Asiago cheese. Bake 2 more minutes or until cheese melts.

Spoon 1 tablespoon squash mixture onto each cheese crouton. Place on a serving tray, and garnish, if desired.
Yield: 4 dozen.

78

VENISON MEATBALLS IN DRIED CHERRY SAUCE

1 pound ground venison
1 pound ground beef
2 teaspoons salt
2 teaspoons freshly ground pepper
1½ teaspoons ground allspice
¼ cup minced onion
3 cloves garlic, minced
2 tablespoons chopped fresh parsley
2 teaspoons chopped fresh thyme
1 large egg, lightly beaten
1 egg white, lightly beaten
3 tablespoons vegetable oil
1 small onion, chopped
1 stalk celery, chopped
2 cloves garlic, chopped
2 tablespoons tomato paste
3 (3-ounce) packages dried cherries
1 bay leaf
5 black peppercorns
2 sprigs fresh thyme
2 teaspoons salt
1 cup Merlot
3 tablespoons balsamic vinegar
2 (14.5-ounce) cans beef broth

Crumble ground venison and ground beef into bowl of a heavy-duty mixer; sprinkle with 2 teaspoons salt, pepper, and allspice. Add ¼ cup onion and next 5 ingredients; mix thoroughly at low speed. Shape mixture into 1" meatballs.

Heat oil in a large skillet over medium-high heat until hot. Add meatballs in batches, and cook until browned, turning often. Remove meatballs from skillet with a slotted spoon; set aside and keep warm.

Cook chopped onion and celery in pan drippings until golden. Add chopped garlic; cook 30 seconds. Reduce heat to medium; stir in tomato paste. Cook until paste begins to brown. Stir in cherries and next 6 ingredients; cook over medium-high heat, scraping bits that cling to bottom of skillet. Bring mixture to a boil, and cook until liquid is reduced by about half. Add broth; return to a boil and cook 15 minutes or until liquid is reduced to 2 cups. Remove from heat; cool slightly, and discard bay leaf and thyme sprigs.

Pour sauce into container of an electric blender; cover and process until smooth, stopping once to scrape down sides. Pour mixture back into skillet through a wire-mesh strainer. Add meatballs to cherry sauce. Bring sauce to a boil; reduce heat and cook, stirring occasionally, until meatballs are thoroughly heated. Transfer meatballs and sauce to a chafing dish. Serve warm with wooden picks. **Yield:** about 4 dozen.

CURRIED CHICKEN TURNOVERS

3 cups all-purpose flour
2 teaspoons curry powder
½ teaspoon salt
¾ cup cold butter, cut into pieces
1 large egg, lightly beaten
¼ cup whipping cream
1 medium onion, quartered
3 cloves garlic, halved
1 (2") piece of ginger, peeled and chopped
1 tablespoon vegetable oil
2 tablespoons curry powder
3 cups finely chopped cooked chicken
½ cup golden raisins
¾ cup whipping cream
½ teaspoon salt
1 large egg, lightly beaten

Pulse first 3 ingredients in a food processor 3 or 4 times or until combined. Add butter; process until mixture is crumbly. With processor running, add 1 egg and ¼ cup cream through food chute; process until dough forms a ball and leaves sides of bowl. Divide dough into thirds, and flatten each portion to a 6" disk; cover and chill 1 hour.

Pulse onion, garlic, and ginger in food processor until minced. Sauté onion mixture in oil in a large skillet over medium-high heat, 5 minutes, or until browned. Stir in 2 tablespoons curry powder, and cook 1 minute. Stir in chicken, raisins, and ¾ cup water. Reduce heat to medium; cover and simmer 10 minutes. Add ¾ cup whipping cream and ½ teaspoon salt. Simmer, uncovered, 3 to 5 minutes or until mixture is thickened. Remove from heat; cool.

Roll each portion of dough into ⅛" thickness on a lightly floured surface; cut with a 3½" round cutter. Place rounds on greased baking sheets.

Spoon 1 tablespoon chicken mixture onto half of each dough circle. Moisten edges with water, and fold dough over filling. Press edges with a fork to seal; prick tops with fork. Combine 1 egg and 1 tablespoon water; beat with a wire whisk. Brush turnovers with egg wash.

Bake at 425° for 8 to 10 minutes or until golden. Serve warm with chutney. **Yield:** about 3 dozen.

MINI PORK SANDWICHES

2 tablespoons chopped fresh rosemary
1½ tablespoons black peppercorns, crushed
1 teaspoon salt
3 pounds pork tenderloins
2 tablespoons olive oil
½ cup mayonnaise
2 tablespoons prepared horseradish
1 tablespoon brandy
1 clove garlic, minced
½ cup Dijon mustard
3 tablespoons capers, chopped
Several bunches arugula
Sweet gherkin pickles, thinly sliced
40 party rolls or small square dinner rolls (we tested with
    Pepperidge Farm country-style soft dinner rolls)

Combine rosemary, crushed peppercorns, and salt. Rub
mixture over tenderloins. Fold thin end under each ten-
derloin; secure with wooden picks. Place tenderloins on a
lightly greased rack in a broiler pan. Drizzle with olive oil.
Bake at 375° for 25 to 30 minutes or until a meat thermometer inserted in thickest part registers 160° (medium).
Let stand 5 minutes. Thinly slice tenderloins.

Combine mayonnaise and next 3 ingredients. Combine
mustard and capers. Spoon sauces into separate serving
bowls. Serve pork with sauces, arugula, gherkins, and rolls
for making do-it-yourself sandwiches. **Yield:** 40 appetizers.

MULLED BLACK CHERRY WINE

*For this mulled wine, select a Cabernet that hints of black
cherry flavor. Labels typically describe a wine's characteristics.*

2 quarts black cherry juice (we tested with R. W. Knudsen
    Family)
3 (3") sticks cinnamon
6 whole cloves
2 (6-ounce) cans pineapple juice
1 (6") piece of ginger, peeled and sliced
⅔ cup sugar
1 (750-milliliter) bottle Cabernet Sauvignon
⅓ cup lime juice

Combine first 6 ingredients in a Dutch oven. Bring to
a boil; cover, reduce heat, and simmer 30 minutes. Stir in
wine and lime juice; heat thoroughly, but do not boil.
Transfer mixture to a heatproof punch bowl, if desired.
Discard whole spices. Serve warm. **Yield:** 13 cups.

Venison Meatballs in
Dried Cherry Sauce

Curried Chicken
Turnovers

HEARTY
HORS D'OEUVRES AFFAIR
menu for 15 to 20

- Sherried Mushroom Spread
  melba toast rounds or crostini
- Eggplant and Walnut Dip
  pita bread, pumpernickel
- Venison Meatballs in Dried
  Cherry Sauce
- Curried Chicken Turnovers
- Mini Pork Sandwiches
- Mulled Black Cherry Wine
- Assorted soft drinks and other
  beverages

Sherried
Mushroom
Spread

Eggplant and
Walnut Dip

Mulled Black
Cherry Wine

Mini Pork
Sandwiches

WHITE HOT CHOCOLATE

Subtle scents of orange and nutmeg waft through the air when you sip this smooth hot chocolate. Serve it with a selection from our cookies chapter.

12 ounces white chocolate, chopped (we tested with Ghirardelli)
1¾ cups whipping cream, divided
6 cups milk
2 tablespoons plus 1 teaspoon orange zest, divided
¼ cup sugar
½ teaspoon vanilla extract
⅛ teaspoon ground nutmeg
Garnish: orange zest

Melt white chocolate in top of a double boiler over hot, not boiling, water.

Combine 1 cup whipping cream, milk, 2 tablespoons orange zest, and sugar in a large saucepan. Bring just to a boil, stirring often. Reduce heat and simmer 2 minutes. Add 1 cup milk mixture to white chocolate in double boiler, stirring well with a wire whisk. Pour white chocolate mixture into milk mixture in saucepan. Cook over low heat until thoroughly heated, stirring gently. Pour into mugs.

Beat remaining ¾ cup whipping cream, 1 teaspoon orange zest, vanilla, and nutmeg at medium speed of an electric mixer until soft peaks form. Spoon dollops of whipped cream onto hot chocolate; garnish, if desired. **Yield:** 9 cups.

SPICED HOT BUTTERED RUM PUNCH

Pull out your favorite holiday mugs and a jar of cinnamon sticks for this classic. Small servings will warm your guests nicely.

½ cup butter, softened
½ cup firmly packed brown sugar
½ teaspoon ground cloves
½ teaspoon ground cinnamon
½ teaspoon vanilla extract
3½ cups boiling water
1¼ cups spiced rum
Garnish: 3" cinnamon sticks

Combine first 5 ingredients in a small bowl, stirring until smooth. Cover and chill until ready to serve.

To serve, combine butter mixture, boiling water, and rum in a small punch bowl, stirring until butter mixture melts. Serve warm with cinnamon-stick stirrers, if desired. **Yield:** 5½ cups.

LEMON FONDUE

Whereas melted chocolate is typically blended with cream and liqueur, we've concocted a luscious lemon version of this popular dessert fondue. Pears and gingersnaps are a must for dipping.

1 (11¼-ounce) jar lemon curd
⅓ cup sweetened condensed milk
¼ cup half-and-half
Garnish: lemon zest

Combine first 3 ingredients in a small bowl, and stir well. Spoon into a footed serving dish. Serve with fresh fruit, gingersnaps, and pound cake cubes. Garnish dish, if desired. **Yield:** 2 cups.

Lemon
Fondue

Caramel-Almond Tartlets

CARAMEL-ALMOND TARTLETS

These petite tarts have a thick shortbread crust and a chewy caramel top.

1¼ cups unbleached all-purpose flour
2 tablespoons brown sugar
¾ teaspoon salt
½ cup cold butter, cut into pieces
1 egg yolk
1 tablespoon whipping cream
1 teaspoon vanilla extract
¾ cup sugar
¾ cup whipping cream
½ teaspoon almond extract
1 cup sliced almonds

Process first 3 ingredients in a food processor just until blended. Add pieces of butter, pulsing 5 or 6 times or until mixture is crumbly.

Combine egg yolk, whipping cream, and vanilla; stir well. With processor running, slowly add egg mixture through food chute; process just until ingredients form a ball and leave sides of bowl. Shape dough into a flat disc; cover and chill 30 minutes.

Place ¾ cup sugar in a large, heavy skillet. Cook over medium heat, stirring constantly with a wooden spoon, until sugar melts and syrup is golden. Remove from heat, and slowly add ¾ cup cream, stirring gently. (Sugar may crack and harden, but will melt again.) Return to heat, and cook, stirring gently, until mixture is smooth and thickened. Remove from heat; stir in almond extract and sliced almonds. Cool.

Cut chilled dough in half; divide each half into 8 balls. Press each ball into a lightly greased 1½" round tartlet pan; place tartlet pans on a baking sheet. Bake at 350° for 12 minutes. Cool slightly.

Increase oven temperature to 400°. Fill each tartlet shell with 1 tablespoon almond filling. Bake at 400° for 14 to 18 minutes or until golden. Cool completely on a wire rack. Remove from pans. **Yield:** 16 tartlets.

Note: For variety, we baked some of the tartlets in 4" x 2" barquette (boat-shaped) molds. We reduced the baking times for the crust and tartlets each to 9 minutes.

CANDLE SLEEVES Create designer table decorations from scented candles that you buy at the grocery store. Cut a piece of sheer or mesh-like fabric slightly wider and twice as tall as a candle in a glass cylinder. Fold the fabric in half lengthwise. Use Heat 'n Bond or a similar product to adhere the side and bottom seams. Place the candle in the sleeve. Tie cording around the candle and sleeve, and loosely fold the excess fabric over the cording to make a puffy collar.

SET FOR THE SEASON

Each season we love to have something new for the table or sideboard. Following are a few suggestions that are sure to be admired by family and friends alike.

MAKE-IT-YOURSELF SIDEBOARD

This table is a great stand-in for a sideboard. It's attractive enough to leave up year-round, but it's also easy to take down and store for special occasions, if desired.

To make the table, cut a piece of ¾" plywood 60" x 18" for the tabletop (a lumberyard can cut the wood for you). The wooden top is supported by two serving tray stands. Tray stands can be purchased (or rented) from a restaurant-supply store. The ones we used are 32" high, and our hem measurements are based on that height. If your table supports are a different height, you will need to adjust the hem accordingly.

For the skirt, we used 5½ yards of burlap. The fabric needs to be at least 63" wide; otherwise 7⅓ yards is required. From the burlap, fold up 6" along one selvage edge to make a hem. Press. Using fabric glue along the top edge, glue the hem in place. From the bottom of the hem, measure and cut at 32¾". Fold under the raw edge at the top ¾", and press.

To make the corner pleats, find the lengthwise center of the fabric and mark this center point on the top edge of the fabric. From this center point, measure 30" and mark. (This is one outside corner.) To create 7"-deep corner pleats, measure and mark (from the corner mark) at 7", 14", 21", and 28". Fold and press on the corner mark the 7", 21", and 28" marks. Press the pleats the full length of the skirt. For the back corner pleat, from the corner, measure and mark at 18", 25", and 32". Press in the pleats at the 18" and 25" marks. The remaining fabric is wrapped to the back side. Repeat the process for the opposite end of the table.

To cover the tabletop, from the remaining fabric, cut a piece of fabric 66" x 24". (Note: If the fabric is open weave, you may want to cut a 66" x 24" piece of muslin to line the fabric.) On a large working surface, place the burlap, the muslin (optional), and the plywood, in that order, taking care to center the wood on the fabric. Wrap the fabric to the wrong side and staple in place, folding excess fabric neatly in place at the corners. Place the tabletop on the tray stands. Find and mark (on the edge) the center on one long side of the tabletop. Match this

MOSS-COVERED CANDLE POTS

With a few inexpensive materials, you can make handsome candleholders that are versatile enough to go from the sideboard to the dining table to the mantel.

Wrap terra-cotta pots with sheet moss, gluing at intervals to help hold the moss in place. Wind cording, twine, or ribbon around the moss-covered pots. Place a large pillar candle in the top, and tuck moss around the candle to conceal the opening.

center mark to the center mark on the skirt. Using push pins or staples, temporarily tack in place, making sure that the center and corners match up. Align the top edge of the hem fold close to the top of the wood edge. Staple the skirt in place on the front and side edges of the tabletop, stapling the corner pleats into place, and wrapping the excess length to the back side. Staple or hot-glue tassels at the corners, if desired. Cover the line of staples by hot-gluing decorative trim over the staples, aligning the top edge of the trim with the top surface of the tabletop.

DINING CHAIR WRAP

For a quick way to dress your dining chairs for a special occasion, wrap a long length of sheer fabric around the chair back, and secure it either by tying the fabric or cinching it in place with a ribbon. If you like, you can fold the fabric's raw edges in toward the center, alleviating the need to hem. For the decoration shown here, we tied a wide ribbon around the fabric and attached clusters of berries to the bow. (The berries have a wire stem that makes it easy to keep them in place.)

MAGNOLIA CHARGER ▶

Set a festive table using these unusual chargers made from magnolia leaves. To create the chargers, spray magnolia leaves (one at a time) with gold floral spray paint. Immediately after spraying each leaf, brush it with a 2" paintbrush to create a two-tone effect (some of the green should show through). Let the paint dry. With a sponge, dab a little silver acrylic paint on each leaf. Let it dry.

Hot-glue the leaves around a cardboard cake circle (available at baking-supply, discount, and crafts stores). To avoid burning your fingers, press the leaves onto the cardboard with a cloth. The leaves last about a week.

PEAR PLACE CARD HOLDERS

These sweet place card holders are fun to make and will last forever, so you can use them again and again. Just change the ribbons to match the event.

Push a piece of Styrofoam into a small terra-cotta pot. Take a fairly straight twig (from your backyard), and push it into the Styrofoam base. With a craft knife, cut a small hole the size of the twig in the bottom of an artificial pear. Secure the pear on top of the twig. With a craft knife, cut a slit on the back side of the pear, just behind the stem, large enough to hold a paper place card.

Fill the top of the pot with moss, and glue leaves and berries on top of the moss, as desired. Tie ribbon bows around the trunk and stem.

◄ WINE BOTTLE COOLERS

Serve wine in style in a colorful cooler. To make a cooler, you'll need an empty 3-liter plastic soft drink bottle and a 750-milliliter, square-shouldered empty wine bottle.

Cut 5" off the top of the plastic bottle; place the wine bottle inside the plastic bottle. Fill the space between the two bottles with kumquats, cranberries, roses, holly, or garland. Pour distilled water (to keep it clear) over the filled space to 2" from the shoulders of the wine bottle. Place tape across the shoulders of the wine bottle, and secure the tape to the plastic bottle to hold the wine bottle upright in the center of the plastic bottle. Put the plastic bottle in the freezer for 24 hours.

Remove the bottle from the freezer, and let it stand at room temperature for 20 minutes. Remove the tape, and hold the bottle under cool running water to remove the plastic bottle. Fill the wine bottle with hot water, and let it stand 10 minutes. Twist the wine bottle to remove it. Place the cooler in a container to catch drips. The wine bottle cooler will last about 2 hours.

FROSTY FLUTES ▲

These snowflake-bedecked champagne glasses set the mood for fun. With a white opaque paint marker (we used DecoColor), draw this simple snowflake design in a random fashion on inexpensive glassware. If you want to keep the painted design, we suggest handwashing the glasses. Otherwise, you can easily scratch off the paint with your fingernail after the party.

◄ NO-SEW TABLE RUNNER

This table runner is so easy to make, you'll want to have several. To make the table runner, select a fabric and cut it to the desired length. (The one pictured is 82" and required 2¼ yards of fabric, 5 yards of trim, and 2 tassels. Yardage requirements will vary according to length.) Cut the width of the runner approximately 18" to 20", perhaps using the fabric design as a guide to an appealing width. Allow 1" extra on each side to fold under. Taper the ends on a 45° angle.

Fold under 1" on all sides and press. Hot-glue the hem. Attach decorative trim to the outside edges of the runner with hot glue. Hot-glue a tassel on each end, if desired.

TORN-PAPER-DESIGN CHARGER

Making this decoupage plate is child's play. Refer to the photograph to copy our design, or feel free to create your own one-of-a-kind pattern. The key to this plate's artsy style is the crackled paint-look finish of the torn-paper background. To make the background, tear white construction paper in small pieces, approximately 1" square. Using decoupage glue,

completely cover a wooden charger with the torn paper pieces, overlapping the edges to hide the plate. Complete the charger by gluing torn pieces of colored construction paper into the desired design. When finished, cover the plate with a thin coating of glue. To use the charger, place a clear glass plate on top to protect the design.

NAPKIN TIE PLACE FAVORS These napkin holders perform a dual duty: They hold the napkin folded before dinner, and after the meal they're a take-home place favor for guests. The ideas shown below include twig star ornaments, brightly colored acrylic candies, a miniature picture frame ornament, and whimsical *Nutcracker* characters.

TOPIARY TREAT

A yummy edible centerpiece, this chocolate tree consists of a Styrofoam cone decorated with bite-size candies. Brush the cone with melted chocolate candy coating. Drizzle the candies with vanilla-flavored candy coating or commercial frosting that comes in a tube. (It takes approximately 75 candy pieces to cover a 15" cone.)

Attach the candies to the tree using wooden picks. (If you need to shorten the picks, simply cut them with scissors.) Since the icing begins to fade after about 24 hours, you may want to assemble this tree the morning of your party. It takes about 1 hour from start to finish.

CITRUSY STYLE

There's nothing sour about this stack of limes, in fact it's quite merry. Create the pyramid's base by hot-gluing limes into a circle the size of the container opening or plate. Stack and glue limes on top of each row, creating smaller circles as you build upward. Fill in the gaps between the fruit with berries and bells.

Tie jumbo jingle bells on each end of several lengths of ribbon, and drape the ribbons across the top of the lime pyramid, securing them at the pyramid's top with straight pins or tacks. Hide the pins with a bow that you pin or glue to the top.

HOLIDAY GLOW This serene centerpiece rises from humble beginnings. Stack two cake stands, a small one on top of a larger one, and load them with frosted votive holders. Greenery clippings and berries fill in the spaces between the candles. That's it! Avoid using glass stands or plates, as the heat from the candles may cause them to crack or break.

◀ SNOWFLAKE TAGS

Add sparkle and shine to your table and gifts with a snowflake tag. Fold holographic paper in half and then in half again, and trace the pattern from page 168 along the fold. Cut and unfold to make a snowflake. Use thread or fishing line to attach the snowflake to a gift package or a napkin holder.

▲ SNOWFLAKE PLACE CARDS

Bring a wintry look to your table with personalized snowflake place cards. Fold a piece of white paper in half and then in half again. Trace the snowflake pattern from page 168 on the fold and cut it out. Cut a rectangle the same width and twice as long as the snowflake from blue cardstock. Fold the cardstock in half and glue the snowflake to one side. Personalize the place cards using a black pen.

MIXING CHINA If you'd rather not purchase a complete set of Christmas china but would like to show a bit of seasonal spirit in your place settings, buy a set of holiday-motif salad or dessert plates or a few serving pieces, and use these with your everyday china. The examples below show how just one dish can set a festive mood.

RIBBON-LACED LINENS

Add holiday flair to table linens by weaving organdy ribbon through the hemstitched borders. Measure the length and width of the napkin or place mat to determine the amount of ribbon needed, adding a few inches to the total to allow for fullness. Using a large needle, pull ribbon through the holes, creating little poufs—but don't pull too tight. To finish, fold the ends under and stitch them together or tie them in a knot. Wash in cold water on the gentle cycle, and lay flat to dry. Press linen when damp, being careful to avoid the ribbon.

ALL THE TRIMMINGS

From selecting the perfect tree to decorating it, much consideration goes into creating your home's focal point during Christmas.

INDULGE IN ORNAMENTS

Make unique ones by hand or select exquisite designs to add to your collection. Display these little jewels all through the house, not just on the tree.

ORNAMENTS ON DISPLAY
Treat favorite Christmas ornaments as works of art, stacking them in creative containers for a seasonal decoration that fits in any room.

◀ For a simple arrangement, place ornaments that are too heavy to hang on the tree in a terra-cotta pot. Give the pot a festive touch by sponging it with gold paint. If you don't have enough ornaments to fill the pot, stuff tissue paper underneath for filler.

▶ A lustrous silver bowl sitting atop a cake stand creates a dramatic setting for metallic-hued Christmas balls. Shiny fabric and ornaments scattered around the base of the bowl give the grouping a heightened presence.

TO MAKE APPLE ORNAMENTS
Shape a Styrofoam ball until it looks like an apple. Using straight pins, attach small red sequins to the ball, overlapping the sequins until the apple is completely covered. Cut a piece of thin cording, and fold it to make a loop. Pin the loop to the top of the ball to form a hanger. Paint the straight pin heads with red paint so they blend in with the sequins. Tack a silk leaf and stem to the top of the ball to complete the apple.

WOODEN FINIAL ORNAMENTS

Home-improvement stores contain tons of ideas for creating ornaments. Purchase a wooden finial from the window treatment department, and paint it gold. Using a smaller brush, paint other colors and designs on the ornament as desired. Turn it upside down so the top is a flat surface. Screw a hook into the top, and tie a ribbon through it to make a hanger.

This ornament makes an attractive adornment hanging from an overhead light, or attach several to hang from an evergreen garland.

FANCY FABRIC ORNAMENTS

For a delightfully detailed ornament, cover a Styrofoam ball with fabric and trims. A bowl filled with these makes an elegant centerpiece.

Tack fabric to a ball with straight pins and then wrap ribbon around it, being sure to cover the pin heads. Use pins to anchor the ribbon at the top and the base of the ball. Further embellish the ornaments with rickrack or cording.

Styrofoam balls come in various sizes, so experiment with smaller and larger ones. If you cover a large ball with fabric, it could even be used as a kissing ball. See pages 66-67 for more kissing ball ideas.

INITIAL ORNAMENTS ▶

Create a personalized ornament to hang from a tree or wreath, or as shown here, use it as an elegant package topper.

Cut 20-gauge wire to the length of the desired finished ornament, and make a loop at one end with pliers. Slide pearl beads on the wire, and finish the other end with a loop. Using the alphabet on page 169 (enlarging the pattern on a copier if necessary), shape the wire to form the letter of your choice. It may be easier to use more than one piece of wire for some letters. Attach multiple pieces together with wire.

◀ BEADED ORNAMENTS

For easy yet dazzling decorations, make these shimmering spherical ornaments. Stack several kinds of beads, from smallest to largest, on a straight pin and attach them to a Styrofoam ball until the surface is completely covered. For variety, combine beads with different colors and shapes. Using a straight pin, attach a ribbon to the top of the ball to form a hanger.

These beaded beauties create a dramatic effect whether hanging on a tree or piled high in a decorative container.

TREE SKIRTS

*Complete your tree's look with a fashionable covering at its base,
continuing the decorating theme all the way to the floor.*

◄ FABRIC NO-SEW TREE SKIRT

Make a tree skirt to suit the style of your tree and home. Choose a heavier-weight fabric, and cut a circle to form the tree skirt. (Figure approximately 1½ yards of 54"-wide fabric for a 54" circle.) Cut a smaller circle in the middle of the fabric for the center opening. Cut a slit from the outer edge to the center opening.

Turn under all raw edges on the skirt, and hem with a glue gun. Attach cording and fringe trim to the outer edge of the skirt with a glue gun.

RIBBON AND TULLE TREE SKIRT ▲

Fashion a soft, romantic look with a tulle, crinoline-like tree skirt. Layer several 2-yard lengths of tulle, one on top of the other. Treating the layers as one piece, fold the tulle in half lengthwise, and stitch 1" from the fold to form a casing. Cut long ribbon streamers; tack one end to the back side of the casing seam, allowing the ribbon to fall loose on top of the skirt. Slide cording through the casing to gather the skirt around the tree's trunk (it should resemble a tutu). Tie the cording to hold the skirt in place.

TREE TREE SKIRT

Ivory-colored wool has a wintry look but also a warm feel to it. This dense fabric makes a wonderful blanket to wrap around the tree's base.

From wool, cut a large circle to form the tree skirt. (Figure approximately 1½ yards of 54"-wide fabric for a 54" circle.) Cut a smaller circle in the middle of the fabric for the center opening. Cut a slit from the outer edge to the center opening. Fold the edges of the slit and inner circle under; press and hem.

Using the tree pattern on page 168, cut trees from remnants of the wool fabric. With green thread, machine-stitch around the trees to finish the edges. Sew a small pearl bead to the tip of each branch and a larger bead on the treetop. Referring to the photograph, arrange the trees on the skirt. Starting at the center bottom of each tree, make a narrow zigzag stitch 1½" long (from the bottom of the tree toward the top). Tack the treetop in place. The sides of the trees remain unattached.

From satin, cut bias strips, and sew them together to form one long piece. With wrong sides together, fold in half lengthwise and press. Stitch the bias strip to the wrong side of the outer edge of the skirt. Press down, then fold the bias strip to the right side and press. Stitch the bias strip to the right side of the skirt to finish. (As an alternative, use purchased bias tape, or machine-stitch the skirt edge to finish.)

OTHER IDEAS FOR TREE SKIRTS

• Arrange a bright quilt around the bottom of the tree for a folk art look.

• An old bedspread, chenille throw, or afghan made in Christmas colors also work well.

• A red, green, or plaid flannel sheet gives a cozy, country feel.

• Try flea-market finds such as old velvet or brocade draperies.

• Bunch long lengths of tulle to form "clouds" around the tree.

BUYING THE TREE

*Trees come in a variety of shapes, sizes, colors, and scents.
Getting home with just the right one can make all the difference.*

Make the selection of the Christmas tree a fun family event, and it will become a favorite ritual each holiday season.

- Consider the scale of the room in your home where you will put the tree. Measure the floor space and height of the ceiling so you'll be prepared at the tree lot.
- Be sure to choose a fresh tree. To determine if a tree is dried out, shake it or run your hand down a branch to see if a lot of needles fall out.
- Once you select the right tree, get it home safely. Make sure you anchor the tree to the roof of the vehicle with rope. You might also want to bring a sheet or plastic to put on the roof of the car to prevent scratches.
- After you get home with the tree, make a fresh cut at its base so it will absorb water faster, and keep the well in the stand filled with water.

GREENERY CHART

The photographs here show branches of four popular types of Christmas trees. Other best-selling varieties include Scotch pine, noble fir, Virginia pine, Leyland cypress, red cedar, and balsam fir.

Fraser fir

The dark blue-green Fraser fir has good needle retention and a pleasant scent.

Spruce

One of the best attributes of the spruce is its naturally symmetrical shape.

Douglas fir

Fir trees are among the most fragrant. The needles smell sweet even when crushed.

White pine

This pine has a full appearance and holds its needles throughout the season but has little to no fragrance.

A Taste of the Season

*Friends, family, and food are the basic elements
for festive holiday gatherings. With these delicious
menus and recipes, the work's easily done.*

VEGETARIAN CHRISTMAS DINNER

This feast of flavors and textures begins with a beautiful beet salad and ends with little cups of incredible chocolate pudding. The center of the plate holds a jumbo mushroom cap topped with mashed potatoes and gravy. No turkey needed.

Menu for 6

Beet Salad with Curried Walnuts • French Onion Soup with Gruyère Toast

Yukon Gold Mash with Morel Sauce • Roasted Brussels Sprouts and Carrots

Chocolate-Cardamom Pudding

Yukon Gold Mash
with Morel Sauce

Roasted Brussels
Sprouts and Carrots

Beet Salad with Curried Walnuts

reduce heat, and simmer 35 to 40 minutes or until tender. Drain; rinse with cold water, and drain again. Trim stems and roots, and rub off skins. Cut beets into 1" pieces.

Combine minced shallot and next 4 ingredients in a large bowl. Add beets; toss. Cover and chill 1 hour.

Melt butter in a skillet over medium heat. Add curry powder, sugar, and ¼ teaspoon salt; cook 1 minute. Add walnuts, and cook, stirring constantly, 2 minutes.

Toss greens in olive oil; divide among 6 plates. Top with beet salad and curried walnuts. **Yield:** 6 servings.

FRENCH ONION SOUP WITH GRUYÈRE TOAST

Fresh mushrooms contribute an earthy essence to the light broth for this soup. Gruyère is a rich, nutty-flavored Swiss cheese that's often melted atop French onion soup.

3 tablespoons olive oil, divided
2 medium onions, sliced
2 cups coarsely chopped mushrooms
1 cup dry white wine (we tested with Chardonnay)
3 (14¼-ounce) cans vegetable broth
3 sprigs fresh parsley
3 sprigs fresh thyme
1 bay leaf
½ teaspoon salt
3 medium onions, sliced
6 (1"-thick) slices baguette
Butter or margarine
4 ounces Gruyère cheese, thinly sliced
¼ teaspoon freshly ground pepper

Heat 2 tablespoons oil in a large skillet over medium-high heat until hot. Add 2 sliced onions and mushrooms; cook 5 minutes, stirring often. Reduce heat to medium; cook 15 minutes or until onion is browned. Add wine, and simmer 2 minutes. Add broth and next 4 ingredients. Bring to a boil; reduce heat, and simmer, partially covered, 30 minutes. Strain broth, discarding solids. Set broth aside.

Heat a large saucepan over medium heat until hot; add remaining 1 tablespoon oil. Add remaining 3 sliced onions, and sauté 10 minutes or until tender. Add reserved broth; cover, reduce heat, and simmer 25 minutes.

Toast baguette slices. Butter each slice and top with cheese; place on a baking sheet. Broil 3" from heat just until cheese melts.

Ladle soup into 6 serving bowls, and top with Gruyère toast. Sprinkle with pepper. Serve hot. **Yield:** 6½ cups.

BEET SALAD WITH CURRIED WALNUTS

Curry and mint are the flavor highlights in this jewel-toned beet salad. You can cook the beets, marinate them in the dressing, and prepare the curried walnuts up to a day ahead.

4 medium beets (1¼ pounds)
2 shallots, minced
¼ cup mirin (rice wine)
2 tablespoons chopped fresh mint
3 tablespoons fresh lemon juice
½ teaspoon salt
1 tablespoon butter or margarine
2 teaspoons curry powder
1 tablespoon sugar
¼ teaspoon salt
½ cup walnut halves, toasted and coarsely chopped
3 cups arugula, watercress or other greens
1 tablespoon olive oil

Trim beets, leaving roots and 1" stems. Scrub beets with a vegetable brush. Place beets in a medium saucepan; add water to cover. Bring to a boil; cover,

YUKON GOLD MASH WITH MOREL SAUCE

This alluring entrée has three parts: a roasted mushroom cap as its base, a buttery mashed potato middle, and an unctuous mushroom sauce that's like meat—which, by the way, you won't miss.

Morel Sauce
6 medium Yukon gold potatoes, peeled and coarsely chopped (2½ pounds)
Roasted Portobello Caps
2 cloves garlic, sliced
¼ cup butter or margarine, melted
1¼ cups milk
1 teaspoon salt
½ teaspoon freshly ground pepper
Garnish: fresh thyme sprigs

Prepare Morel Sauce.

Cook chopped potatoes in boiling salted water to cover 20 minutes or until tender. Drain potatoes, and set aside.

Meanwhile, prepare Roasted Portobello Caps.

Sauté garlic in butter in a large saucepan over medium heat until butter and garlic are golden. Add milk, salt, and pepper. Bring to a simmer; remove from heat, and add potatoes. Mash with a potato masher until almost smooth.

To serve, spoon Yukon Gold Mash into Roasted Portobello Caps; top with Morel Sauce. Garnish, if desired. **Yield:** 6 servings.

MOREL SAUCE

3 (½-ounce) packages dried morel mushrooms, rinsed and drained
2 cups boiling water
2 tablespoons butter or margarine
2 tablespoons olive oil
2 cups coarsely chopped fresh mushrooms (8 ounces)
¾ cup finely chopped onion
¾ cup port wine
2 tablespoons balsamic vinegar
¼ cup all-purpose flour
½ cup water
½ cup half-and-half
1½ tablespoons chopped fresh sage
1 teaspoon salt
½ teaspoon freshly ground pepper

Place morels in 2 cups boiling water; let stand 5 minutes. Remove morels with a slotted spoon, reserving broth. Strain broth, discarding any sandy residue in bottom of pan. Chop morels. Set morels and broth aside.

Heat butter and oil in a large, deep skillet over medium-high heat until butter melts. Add fresh mushrooms and onion. Cook, stirring constantly, 5 minutes or until onion is browned; add morels, wine, and vinegar. Reduce heat, and simmer, uncovered, 2 minutes. Add reserved broth; bring to a boil, reduce heat, and simmer, uncovered, 3 minutes.

Combine flour and water, stirring until smooth. Add to mushroom mixture. Cook, stirring constantly, 2 minutes or until thickened and smooth. Stir in half-and-half and remaining ingredients. Cook 5 minutes. Serve over Yukon Gold Mash. **Yield:** 4 cups.

ROASTED PORTOBELLO CAPS

6 portobello mushroom caps
3 to 4 tablespoons olive oil
1 teaspoon salt
1 teaspoon freshly ground pepper

Place mushroom caps in a large bowl. Drizzle with oil and sprinkle with seasonings. Toss gently, being careful not to tear mushrooms. Arrange mushrooms, cavity side down, in a single layer in a jellyroll pan or shallow roasting pan.

Roast at 450° for 15 minutes, turning once. **Yield:** 6 servings.

ROASTED BRUSSELS SPROUTS AND CARROTS

The key to crispy-roasted results here is using a large pan so vegetables aren't crowded during roasting. Roast the vegetables several hours before the meal; then reheat just before serving.

2 pounds fresh brussels sprouts
8 medium carrots, scraped and cut into 2" pieces
¼ cup olive oil
1 tablespoon sugar
1 tablespoon chopped fresh thyme
½ teaspoon salt
Freshly ground pepper

Wash brussels sprouts; remove discolored leaves. Trim ends, and cut in half lengthwise. Cut larger pieces of carrot in half lengthwise, if desired.

Place brussels sprouts and carrots in a large roasting pan. Combine olive oil and remaining ingredients; pour over vegetables, and toss well. Cover and bake at 425° for 20 minutes. Uncover, and roast 25 minutes or until vegetables are tender and well browned, stirring twice. **Yield:** 6 servings.

CHOCOLATE-CARDAMOM PUDDING

This rich pudding has several highlights: silky smooth texture thanks to tofu, a bewitching blend of flavors, and a simple serving suggestion.

1 (12.3-ounce) package soft silken tofu (we tested with Mori-Nu)
½ (14-ounce) can coconut milk (about 1 cup)
2 tablespoons sugar
1½ teaspoons cardamom pods
2 (4-ounce) bars bittersweet chocolate, melted (we tested with Ghirardelli)

Place tofu on several layers of heavy-duty paper towels; cover with additional paper towels and place on a plate. Place a heavy object on top of paper towels; let stand 20 minutes to extract excess liquid.

Place coconut milk, sugar, and cardamom pods in a saucepan; bring to a boil. Cover, reduce heat, and simmer 20 minutes. Remove and discard cardamom pods.

Combine milk mixture, tofu, and melted chocolate in a food processor. Process 2 to 3 minutes or until mixture is smooth and creamy, stopping once to scrape down sides. Spoon mixture into demitasse cups or pots de crème cups. Cover and chill, if desired. **Yield:** 6 servings.

Chocolate-Cardamom Pudding

OF WINE & WINTER HERBS

*Wine and herbs are the essence of many great-tasting meals.
In this menu we honor the sprawling rosemary sprig.
Rosemary's piney fresh flavor is sprinkled throughout these recipes
and matched with rich red wines along the way.*

Menu for 6 to 8

Savory Kalamata Cheesecake Squares • Greens with Black Cherry Dressing

Beef Daube • Crumb-Topped Penne Pasta • Gingerbread Trifle

Greens with Black
Cherry Dressing

SAVORY KALAMATA CHEESECAKE SQUARES

Here's a new twist: cheesecake as the appetizer. Purplish-black olives scatter specks of color into each savory bite. Garnish your platter with herbs and olives so your guests will know it's not dessert. Serve a Pinot Noir with these rich squares.

1¼ cups Italian-seasoned breadcrumbs
½ cup very finely chopped pecans
⅓ cup butter or margarine, melted
1 (8-ounce) package cream cheese, softened
1 (3-ounce) package cream cheese, softened
1 (8-ounce) carton sour cream
1 tablespoon all-purpose flour
¼ teaspoon salt
¼ teaspoon pepper
1 large egg
1 egg yolk
½ cup kalamata olives, pitted and sliced or chopped
1 tablespoon chopped fresh rosemary
Garnishes: fresh rosemary sprigs, kalamata olives

Combine first 3 ingredients; stir well. Press crumb mixture firmly into a lightly greased, foil-lined 9" square pan. Bake at 350° for 12 minutes. Set aside to cool.

Beat cream cheese, sour cream, flour, and seasonings at medium speed of an electric mixer until smooth. Add egg and egg yolk, one at a time, beating just until blended. Stir in sliced olives and chopped rosemary; pour filling into baked crust. Bake at 350° for 20 minutes or just until firm. Cool to room temperature on a wire rack. Cover and chill.

To serve, lift foil out of pan, and cut cheesecake into squares. Garnish serving platter, if desired. **Yield:** 3 dozen.

GREENS WITH BLACK CHERRY DRESSING

In this salad, you'll taste a delicious marriage of flavors as candied nuts, crisp bacon, and Parmesan cheese are tossed with greens and dressed in a wine vinaigrette. For the dressing, look for a Pinot Noir whose label boasts notes of black cherry. Then serve the same bottle to start off the meal.

½ cup extra virgin olive oil
3 tablespoons Pinot Noir
1 tablespoon white vinegar
2 teaspoons Dijon mustard
1 small shallot, minced
⅛ teaspoon salt
⅛ teaspoon sugar
⅛ teaspoon freshly ground pepper
6 to 8 cups mixed salad greens
1 (8-ounce) package sliced fresh mushrooms
6 slices bacon, cooked and coarsely crumbled
Candied Walnuts
Freshly shaved Parmesan cheese

Combine first 8 ingredients in a jar. Cover tightly and shake vigorously until blended. Toss greens, mushrooms, and bacon in a salad bowl. Drizzle with dressing; toss gently. Sprinkle with Candied Walnuts and Parmesan cheese. **Yield:** 6 to 8 servings.

CANDIED WALNUTS
⅔ cup sugar
24 walnut halves

Cook sugar in a large, heavy skillet over medium heat, stirring constantly with a wooden spoon, 5 to 10 minutes or until melted and golden.
Turn heat off. Working quickly, drop walnut halves into caramelized sugar, 4 at a time, turning to coat. Using a fork, remove walnuts to wax paper to cool. **Yield:** 24 pieces.

Savory Kalamata
Cheesecake Squares

Crumb-Topped
Penne Pasta

Beef Daube

BEEF DAUBE

Daube, a French country stew, is a homey dish made from simple ingredients. The secret to its rich flavor is to cook and cool it over a two-day period—a real bonus if you're enter-taining and looking for make-ahead menu options.

¼ cup olive oil or vegetable oil
1 (4-pound) boneless rump roast or chuck roast, well trimmed and cut into 2" pieces
1½ teaspoons salt
1½ teaspoons freshly ground pepper
4 small yellow onions, cut into wedges
4 large carrots, scraped and cut into 2" pieces
1 head garlic, separated into cloves, each peeled and halved lengthwise
1 (14½-ounce) can Italian stewed tomatoes
1 (750-milliliter) bottle Cabernet Sauvignon or Côtes du Rhône or other spicy, full-bodied red wine
Bouquet garni*
Garnish: fresh rosemary

Heat oil in a Dutch oven over medium heat until hot. Sprinkle beef with salt and pepper. Brown beef in several batches in hot oil until browned on all sides. Remove beef to a large plate, reserving drippings in Dutch oven.

Sauté onion, carrot, and garlic in reserved drippings over medium heat 6 to 8 minutes. Add tomatoes and wine. Return beef to pan; add bouquet garni. Bring to a boil; cover, reduce heat, and simmer 1½ hours. Remove from heat, and cool completely. Cover pan and refrigerate overnight.

Remove Dutch oven from refrigerator. Skim fat from surface, if desired. Let stew stand 20 minutes. Bring to a boil over medium heat; cover, reduce heat, and simmer 1 hour. Uncover and simmer 30 more minutes or until beef is very tender and stew is thickened. Discard bouquet garni before serving. Garnish each serving, if desired.
Yield: 6 to 8 servings.

*A bouquet garni *is a small bundle of fresh herbs, such as parsley, thyme, and bay leaves, tied together with kitchen twine. We tested with flat-leaf parsley, rosemary, and 2 bay leaves.*

118

CRUMB-TOPPED PENNE PASTA

This version of the French macaronade, a traditional accompaniment to Beef Daube, uses penne pasta instead of macaroni. The ridged pasta is meant to soak up the daube's brown gravy.

8 ounces penne pasta
1 cup freshly shredded Parmesan cheese
1½ cups soft French breadcrumbs, lightly toasted (homemade)
3 to 4 tablespoons butter or margarine, melted

Cook pasta in salted water according to package directions; drain, reserving ⅓ cup pasta water. Toss cooked pasta with reserved pasta water; cool slightly. Stir in cheese. Spoon pasta mixture into a greased oval gratin dish or other shallow small baking dish.

Combine breadcrumbs and melted butter; toss gently. Sprinkle over pasta. Broil 5½" from heat 1 minute or until lightly browned. Serve hot. **Yield:** 6 to 8 servings.

GINGERBREAD TRIFLE

Pair homemade gingerbread with custard, and you get this fabulous dessert that can be made earlier in the day. For a shortcut, prepare gingerbread from a packaged mix. You can also use commercial vanilla pudding as a stand-in for our wonderfully thick custard.

½ cup butter or margarine, softened
½ cup firmly packed dark brown sugar
1 large egg
1 cup molasses
2½ cups all-purpose flour
1 tablespoon ground ginger
2 teaspoons baking powder
½ teaspoon baking soda
½ teaspoon salt
¼ teaspoon freshly ground pepper
1 cup hot water
Custard
2 cups frozen whipped topping, thawed
4 (1.4-ounce) English toffee-flavored candy bars, coarsely chopped

Beat butter at medium speed of an electric mixer until creamy. Gradually add sugar, beating until light and fluffy. Add egg and molasses, mixing well.

Combine flour and next 5 ingredients; add to butter mixture alternately with water, beginning and ending with flour mixture. Beat at low speed after each addition until blended. Pour batter into a greased 13" x 9" pan.

Bake at 350° for 30 to 35 minutes or until a wooden pick inserted in center comes out clean. Cool in pan on a wire rack.

Cut gingerbread into cubes. Arrange one-third of gingerbread cubes in a 3-quart trifle bowl; top with one-third of Custard. Repeat layers twice, ending with Custard. Cover and chill until ready to serve.

Before serving, spread whipped topping over trifle. Sprinkle with chopped candy bars. **Yield:** 10 servings.

CUSTARD

1⅓ cups sugar
⅔ cup all-purpose flour
½ teaspoon salt
5 cups milk
6 egg yolks, lightly beaten
1 tablespoon vanilla extract or dark rum

Combine first 3 ingredients in a large heavy saucepan; whisk in milk. Cook over medium heat, stirring constantly, until thickened and bubbly. Gradually stir about one-fourth of hot mixture into egg yolks; add to remaining hot mixture, stirring constantly. Cook over medium heat, stirring constantly, 3 minutes. Remove from heat; add vanilla. Cool to room temperature. Assemble trifle, or cover and chill custard until ready for assembly. **Yield:** 5 cups.

Gingerbread
Trifle

ENTERTAINING FRIENDS

This elegant meal delivers flavor and presentation. Several elements of the menu can be made ahead, giving you time to focus on special touches for the evening. Turn to our Great Party Tips to get ideas and inspiration for your next gathering.

Menu for 6

Endive Salad with Pancetta • Pecan-Crusted Rack of Lamb

Roasted Vegetables • Smoked Mozzarella Bread Puddings • Pear Frangipan Tart

Endive Salad with Pancetta

ENDIVE SALAD WITH PANCETTA

This salad showcases several wonderful ingredients: slender heads of pale green endive, salty Italian bacon, and bold blue cheese. Use the whole endive leaves that surround the plate to scoop up the yummy salad toppings.

4 thin slices pancetta or other bacon, chopped
1 shallot, finely chopped
¼ cup mirin (rice wine)
¼ cup sherry wine vinegar
¼ cup canola oil or olive oil
2 heads Belgian endive, julienne-sliced
2 stalks celery, julienne-sliced
1 Red Delicious apple, diced
1½ cups small fresh mushrooms, quartered
2 tablespoons fresh lemon juice
1 head Belgian endive, separated into leaves
½ cup crumbled blue cheese (we tested with Maytag)

Sauté pancetta and shallot in a large skillet over medium heat 5 minutes or until browned. Add mirin and wine vinegar; simmer 2 minutes. Whisk in oil. Set aside, and keep warm.

Combine sliced endive, celery, apple, and mushrooms; sprinkle with lemon juice, and toss well. Arrange salad on individual serving plates. Tuck several endive leaves around edge of each salad. Drizzle with reserved warm dressing, and sprinkle with blue cheese. **Yield:** 6 servings.

Pecan-Crusted Rack of Lamb

Roasted Vegetables

PECAN-CRUSTED RACK OF LAMB

A Dijon mustard coating and pecan crust dress these stately racks for the table.

2 tablespoons Dijon mustard
1 tablespoon lemon juice
1 tablespoon olive oil
½ teaspoon salt
1 tablespoon finely chopped fresh mint or 1 teaspoon
  dried mint
1 tablespoon finely chopped fresh oregano or 1 teaspoon
  dried oregano
2 (8-rib) lamb rib roasts (2¾ to 3 pounds each)
1 cup pecan pieces
¼ teaspoon salt
½ teaspoon freshly ground pepper
2 tablespoons butter or margarine, melted
1 tablespoon lemon juice

Combine first 6 ingredients; stir well. Spread mustard mixture over meaty portion of lamb racks; set aside.

Process pecans in a food processor until ground. Combine pecans, ¼ teaspoon salt, pepper, butter, and 1 tablespoon lemon juice. Pat pecan mixture over mustard-coated lamb.

Place roasts on a rack in a roasting pan, fat side out and ribs crisscrossed. Insert meat thermometer into thickest part of lamb, making sure it does not touch bone. Roast at 425° for 35 to 40 minutes or until thermometer registers 150° (medium-rare). (Cover roasts loosely with foil after 25 minutes, if necessary, to prevent excessive browning.) Let stand 10 minutes before slicing. **Yield:** 6 servings.

Lamb know-how: When you're preparing racks of lamb, let a butcher do some of the work for you. Ask him to french the chine bones (remove fat and gristle) and to trim the cap fat, leaving only the tender eye meat and resulting in a beautiful entrée presentation.

ROASTED VEGETABLES

Roasting emphasizes the natural sweetness in vegetables. High heat creates a caramelized or crisp surface, sealing in flavor. Scatter these colorful roasted chunks on the platter with the rustic lamb.

1½ pounds sweet potatoes, peeled and cut into 1½"
 pieces (2 medium)
¾ pound turnips, peeled and cut into 1½" pieces
 (3 small)
1 large onion, peeled and cut into 1½" wedges
6 cloves garlic, peeled
3 tablespoons olive oil
1 tablespoon chopped fresh rosemary
1 tablespoon chopped fresh oregano or marjoram
1 teaspoon salt

Combine first 5 ingredients in a large bowl; toss well. Arrange vegetables in a single layer in a large roasting pan or broiler pan. Roast at 450° for 25 to 30 minutes or until well browned, stirring gently every 10 minutes. Stir in herbs and salt just before serving. **Yield:** 6 servings.

SMOKED MOZZARELLA BREAD PUDDINGS

The tang of sourdough meets smoked mozzarella cheese in these savory bread puddings that simmer on the stovetop, keeping your oven free to roast the rest of the meal.

9 slices day-old sourdough bread
1½ cups buttermilk
5 egg yolks
1 medium leek, cleaned and sliced
3 tablespoons butter or margarine
1 cup whipping cream
1 cup (4 ounces) shredded smoked mozzarella cheese
½ teaspoon salt
¼ teaspoon pepper

Remove crust from bread; reserve crust for other uses. Cut bread slices in half and place in an 11" x 7" baking dish.

Whisk buttermilk and egg yolks; set aside. Sauté sliced leek in butter in a small skillet over medium heat until tender. Remove from heat; cool. Combine buttermilk mixture, leek, cream, mozzarella cheese, salt, and pepper. Pour over bread. Let stand 20 minutes.

Layer spoonfuls of bread and leek mixture into six (6-ounce) greased ramekins. Place ramekins in a roasting pan, and add hot water to pan to depth of 1½". Place

roasting pan over 2 burners; cover completely with heavy-duty aluminum foil, and cook over medium heat 1 hour or until bread puddings are set. Remove ramekins from roasting pan. Broil just before serving to brown tops, if desired. **Yield:** 6 servings.

Pear Frangipan
Tart

PEAR FRANGIPAN TART

This showy French tart is superb served with vanilla bean ice cream. Frangipan *refers to the buttery ground almond filling.*

½ cup butter, cut into pieces
1½ cups all-purpose flour
¼ teaspoon salt
3 tablespoons ice water
1¼ cups slivered almonds
½ cup sugar
2 tablespoons all-purpose flour
½ cup butter, softened
2 large eggs
2 tablespoons powdered sugar
¼ teaspoon salt
1 cup dry white wine
2 cups water
1 cup sugar
2 teaspoons vanilla extract
3 large Bosc pears, peeled
1 tablespoon butter or margarine, melted
1 tablespoon cornstarch

Pulse first 3 ingredients in a food processor until mixture is crumbly. Slowly add ice water through food chute, pulsing until mixture forms a ball. Flatten dough to a 6" disc; wrap in plastic wrap and chill 1 hour.

Process almonds in food processor until finely ground. Combine almonds, ½ cup sugar, and 2 tablespoons flour in a small bowl; set aside.

Beat softened butter, eggs, powdered sugar, and ¼ teaspoon salt at medium speed of an electric mixer until creamy. Combine almond and butter mixtures. Cover and chill 1 hour.

Roll pastry to ⅛" thickness on a floured surface. Fit pastry into a 10" tart pan; place on a baking sheet. Bake at 425° for 12 minutes. Cool. Reduce oven temperature to 400°.

Combine wine, 2 cups water, 1 cup sugar, and vanilla in a large saucepan; bring just to a boil. Add pears and simmer 8 minutes. Remove from heat. Cool pears completely in liquid. Remove pears and pat dry. Reserve 1 cup poaching liquid.

Cut pears in half vertically, remove cores, and cut pears into ¼" thick lengthwise slices, keeping stem ends intact.

Spread almond mixture into baked tart shell. Arrange sliced pear halves over almond mixture, stem ends toward center. Fan pears slightly. Brush pears with melted butter. Bake at 400° for 30 minutes or until golden.

Combine reserved 1 cup poaching liquid and cornstarch in a small saucepan, stirring until smooth. Cook over medium heat, stirring constantly, until mixture thickens. Boil 1 minute, stirring constantly. Remove from heat. Brush tart with glaze mixture. Remove sides of tart pan before serving. **Yield:** 1 (10") tart.

COOKIE COLLECTION

Bring out the cookie sheets; preheat the oven. It's time for a holiday baking bonanza. The results? Chewy, gooey, fudgy, nutty, crunchy, crispy goodies—cookies to please one and all.

FUDGY JOY COOKIES

Soft, chocolaty cookies still warm from the oven are always a big hit. This recipe will remind you of a popular coconut-almond-chocolate candy bar.

2 cups all-purpose flour
½ cup quick-cooking oats
½ cup cocoa
1 teaspoon baking soda
¼ teaspoon salt
1 cup butter or margarine
3 (1-ounce) squares semisweet chocolate, finely chopped
1 cup sugar
½ cup firmly packed brown sugar
2 large eggs
2 teaspoons vanilla extract
¾ cup finely chopped flaked coconut
½ cup slivered almonds, toasted and coarsely chopped

Combine first 5 ingredients; stir well, and set aside.

Combine butter and chocolate in a small saucepan; cook over low heat, stirring often, until melted and smooth. Remove from heat. Transfer mixture to a large bowl; cool completely.

Add sugars to chocolate mixture, beating at medium speed of an electric mixer until well blended. Add eggs and vanilla; beat until smooth. Gradually add flour mixture, beating well. Stir in coconut and almonds. Cover and chill dough 1 hour.

Drop dough by rounded tablespoonfuls onto ungreased cookie sheets. Bake at 350° for 10 minutes. Cool 1 minute on cookie sheets; remove to wire racks, and cool completely. **Yield:** 3½ dozen.

Two-Tone Cookies: *Fill half of a measuring tablespoon with Fudgy Joy Cookie dough. Press Orange-Macadamia Nut Cookie dough into the other half of spoon. Drop two-toned dough onto ungreased cookie sheet. Repeat procedure with*

remaining dough. Bake at 350° for 10 to 12 minutes. Cool 2 minutes on cookie sheets; remove to wire racks, and cool completely. **Yield:** 6 dozen.

ORANGE-MACADAMIA NUT COOKIES

Macadamia nuts and white chocolate pair up in this delicious drop cookie.

¾ cup butter or margarine, softened
½ cup sugar
½ cup firmly packed brown sugar
1 large egg
1 tablespoon grated orange rind
¾ teaspoon vanilla extract
¼ teaspoon orange extract
1⅓ cups all-purpose flour
½ cup quick-cooking oats
¾ teaspoon baking powder
½ teaspoon baking soda
1 (3.5-ounce) jar lightly salted macadamia nuts, coarsely chopped
1 cup white chocolate morsels or chunks

Beat butter at medium speed of an electric mixer 2 minutes or until creamy. Gradually add sugars, beating well. Add egg, orange rind, and flavorings.

Combine flour and next 3 ingredients. Add to butter mixture, beating at low speed just until blended. Stir in nuts and white chocolate morsels. Cover and chill dough 2 hours.

Drop dough by rounded tablespoonfuls onto ungreased cookie sheets. Bake at 350° for 9 to 10 minutes or just until edges are golden. Cool 1 minute on cookie sheets; remove to wire racks, and cool completely. **Yield:** about 3 dozen.

BUTTERCRISP COOKIES

These crispy-edged cookies have bits of candy in every bite. Baking them on parchment paper helps you easily remove them to wire racks.

¾ cup unsalted butter, softened
¾ cup sugar
¾ cup firmly packed brown sugar
2 large eggs
2¼ cups all-purpose flour
2 teaspoons baking powder
1 teaspoon salt
1 tablespoon vanilla extract
1 (6-ounce) package white chocolate baking squares, coarsely chopped
6 (2.1-ounce) chocolate-covered crispy peanut-buttery candy bars, coarsely chopped
1 cup uncooked regular oats

Beat butter at medium speed of an electric mixer until creamy. Add sugars, beating until fluffy. Add eggs, one at a time, beating just until blended.

Combine flour, baking powder, and salt. Gradually add to butter mixture, beating until blended. Stir in vanilla. Stir in white chocolate, candy, and oats. Cover and chill dough 30 minutes.

Drop dough by heaping teaspoonfuls onto parchment paper-lined cookie sheets. Bake at 350° for 8 to 9 minutes or until golden (do not overbake). Cool 5 minutes on cookie sheets; remove to wire racks, and cool completely. **Yield:** 5 dozen.

CHERRY LEMON CROWNS

The colors of Christmas dot these lightly lemon butter cookies.

⅔ cup butter or margarine, softened
1 (3-ounce) package cream cheese, softened
1 cup sugar
1 egg yolk
1 teaspoon grated lemon rind
1 teaspoon fresh lemon juice
2 cups all-purpose flour
1 dozen each candied red and green cherries, halved
Lemon Glaze

Beat butter and cream cheese at medium speed of an electric mixer until creamy. Gradually add sugar, beating until light and fluffy. Add egg yolk, lemon rind, and lemon juice, beating well. Add flour, beating until blended. Cover and chill dough 2 hours.

Shape dough into 1" balls. Place 2" apart on ungreased cookie sheets. Flatten each ball into a 1½" disc. Press a candied cherry half in center of each cookie.

Bake at 350° for 12 to 15 minutes or until edges are barely golden. Cool 1 minute on cookie sheets; remove to wire racks, and cool completely. Drizzle lightly with Lemon Glaze. Let stand until glaze sets. **Yield:** 4 dozen.

Cherry Lemon Crowns

LEMON GLAZE

1½ cups sifted powdered sugar
1 to 2 tablespoons fresh lemon juice

Combine powdered sugar and lemon juice, stirring well. (Glaze should be thick, yet easy to drizzle.) **Yield:** enough for 4 dozen cookies.

NUTMEG SUGAR COOKIES

Freshly grated nutmeg brings out a delicious difference in these simple old-fashioned cookies.

½ cup butter, softened
1 cup sugar
2 large eggs
½ cup sour cream
1 teaspoon vanilla extract
2¾ cups all-purpose flour
1½ teaspoons baking powder
¼ teaspoon baking soda
¾ teaspoon freshly grated nutmeg
¼ teaspoon salt
⅓ cup sugar
¼ teaspoon freshly grated nutmeg

Beat butter at medium speed of an electric mixer until creamy. Gradually add 1 cup sugar, beating well. Add eggs, sour cream, and vanilla; beat well.

Combine flour, baking powder, soda, ¾ teaspoon nutmeg, and salt; stir well. Gradually add to butter mixture, beating until blended. Cover and chill dough at least 3 hours.

Combine ⅓ cup sugar and remaining ¼ teaspoon nutmeg; stir well. Shape dough into 1" balls. Place 2" apart on lightly greased cookie sheets. Grease bottom of a glass. Dip glass in sugar mixture, and press each ball flat.

Bake at 375° for 8 minutes or until edges are lightly browned. Remove cookies to wire racks immediately to cool. **Yield:** 5 dozen.

PDQ Turtle Cookies

Turtle cookies never tasted so good. The pecan "feet" provide little handles for easy eating.

1 (14-ounce) package caramels (we tested with Farley's)
1 (9-ounce) package chocolate wafer cookies (42 wafers)
3½ cups pecan halves
1 cup ready-to-spread milk chocolate frosting (we tested with Duncan Hines)
Chocolate sprinkles

Unwrap caramels; set aside.

Place half of chocolate wafers, flat side up, on an ungreased cookie sheet. Top each wafer with a caramel. Bake at 350° for 5 minutes or just until caramels are soft. Immediately press 5 pecan halves, flat side up, into each caramel, resembling 4 turtle feet and a head. (Allow pecans to stick out beyond edges of each cookie.) Let cookies cool slightly; remove to wire racks, and cool completely. Repeat procedure with remaining chocolate wafers, caramels, and pecans.

Turn cookies over and spread tops with chocolate frosting; sprinkle with chocolate sprinkles. **Yield:** 3½ dozen.

The fun is in the making when your kids help. Let them frost and decorate each turtle.

129

CHOCOLATE-APRICOT THUMBPRINT COOKIES

Pockets of apricot preserves fill these pecan-coated cookies. A chocolate drizzle dresses them up, but they're just as tempting unadorned. See how we stacked them for gift giving on page 139.

½ cup butter or margarine, softened
½ cup sugar
1 large egg, separated
1 teaspoon vanilla extract
1 cup all-purpose flour
¼ teaspoon salt
2 cups finely chopped pecans, divided
½ cup apricot preserves
½ cup semisweet chocolate morsels, melted

Beat butter at medium speed of an electric mixer until creamy; gradually add sugar, beating until fluffy. Add egg yolk and vanilla; beat well.

Combine flour and salt; add to butter mixture, beating well. Stir in 1 cup pecans. Cover and chill dough at least 30 minutes.

Lightly beat egg white. Shape dough into 1" balls; dip each ball in egg white, and roll in remaining 1 cup pecans. Place balls 1" apart on greased cookie sheets. Press thumb gently into center of each ball, leaving an indention; fill with preserves.

Bake at 350° for 17 to 18 minutes or until lightly browned. Cool 1 minute on cookie sheets; remove to wire racks, and cool completely. Drizzle melted chocolate over cooled cookies, using a fork or spoon. **Yield:** 3 dozen.

Chocolate-Apricot
Thumbprint Cookies

HARVEST BISCOTTI

Mashed sweet potato makes this biscotti stand out in a crowd. For added indulgence, dip one side of each twice-baked log in vanilla-flavored candy coating (see Note).

⅔ cup butter or margarine, softened
⅔ cup sugar
⅔ cup firmly packed brown sugar
4 large eggs
1 cup cooked, mashed sweet potato (1 large sweet potato)
1 teaspoon vanilla extract
4 cups all-purpose flour
1 tablespoon baking powder
¼ teaspoon salt
1 cup finely chopped pecans, toasted

Beat butter at medium speed of an electric mixer until creamy. Gradually add sugars, beating until fluffy. Add eggs, one at a time, beating after each addition. Add sweet potato and vanilla; beat until blended.

Combine flour, baking powder, and salt; add to butter mixture, beating at low speed until blended. Turn dough out onto a lightly floured surface, and knead in pecans. Divide dough in half. Using floured hands, shape each portion into a 10" x 6" log on a lightly greased cookie sheet.

Bake at 375° for 25 minutes. Cool 5 minutes on cookie sheet; remove to a wire rack, and cool to the touch. Reduce oven temperature to 325°.

Cut each log crosswise into ½"-thick slices with a serrated knife. Place slices, cut side down, on ungreased cookie sheets.

Bake at 325° for 15 minutes; turn slices over and bake 15 more minutes. Turn slices upright, and return to oven. Turn oven off, and leave in oven 15 minutes or until dry. Cool completely on wire racks. **Yield:** 2½ dozen.

Note: *You can sweeten the flavor or change the length of this biscotti.*

For a sweeter treat, *dip biscotti in vanilla-flavored candy coating. Here's how: Melt coating, 8 ounces at a time, in an 11" x 7" baking dish in the microwave according to package directions. Dip each biscotti, cut side down, into melted coating. Place biscotti, dipped side up, on wax paper until coating has hardened.*

For long biscotti, *carefully cut each log lengthwise into ½"-thick slices after the first baking.* **Yield:** 1½ dozen.

Harvest Biscotti

GRAHAM STARS

Whole grain, stone-ground flour gives these cookies a nutty aroma and taste. They're crisp and sturdy, ideal for making cookie garlands to take to a cookie swap.

½ cup butter, softened
½ cup firmly packed brown sugar
⅓ cup honey
1 large egg
1 teaspoon vanilla extract
1½ cups all-purpose flour
1 cup whole wheat graham flour
½ teaspoon baking soda
⅛ teaspoon salt
¾ cup sifted powdered sugar
1 teaspoon ground cinnamon

Beat butter at medium speed of an electric mixer until creamy; gradually add brown sugar and honey, beating well. Add egg and vanilla; beat well.

Combine flours, baking soda, and salt; gradually add to butter mixture, beating just until blended. Divide dough into four portions; shape each portion into a disc. Wrap in plastic wrap, and chill dough at least 1 hour.

Working with one portion of dough at a time, roll dough to ⅛" thickness on a lightly floured surface. Cut with a 3" star-shaped cookie cutter. Place cutouts on lightly greased cookie sheets. Using a plastic drinking straw, make a hole in center of each star, and twist the straw to remove tiny piece of dough.

Bake at 375° for 8 minutes or until edges of cookies are lightly browned. Cool slightly on cookie sheets; remove to wire racks, and cool completely. Repeat procedure with remaining portions of dough.

Combine powdered sugar and cinnamon in a large zip-top bag; seal and toss to combine. Add cookies to bag, about 5 at a time, and shake gently to coat. Remove coated cookies from bag, and repeat procedure with remaining cookies. String cookies onto raffia or ribbon, if desired. **Yield:** 4 dozen.

Graham Stars

Use a plastic drinking straw to make holes in center of cookie dough cutouts. After baking and coating cookies with sugar, string them onto desired lengths of knotted ribbon.

MARBLED CINNAMON HEARTS

Here's an art deco cookie as at home for Valentine's Day as it is for Christmas. See it in our cookie box on page 139.

1 recipe Chocolate-Cinnamon Dough
1 recipe Vanilla Dough

Divide both doughs in half. Roll one portion of Chocolate-Cinnamon Dough into a 9" square on a lightly floured surface. Roll one portion of Vanilla Dough into a 9" square, and place on top of chocolate square. Continue rolling and stacking remaining two portions of dough, resulting in a 4-layer stack of alternating dough, pressing layers firmly to adhere.

Tear away a portion of stacked dough, and knead 2 or 3 times. (Too much kneading will prevent marbled look.) Roll dough to 1/8" thickness on a lightly floured surface. Cut with a 3" heart-shaped cookie cutter; place on ungreased cookie sheets. Repeat procedure with remaining dough.

Bake at 350° for 12 minutes or until lightly browned. Cool 1 minute on cookie sheets; remove to wire racks, and cool completely. **Yield:** 6 dozen.

CHOCOLATE-CINNAMON DOUGH

1 cup butter or margarine, softened
1 cup sugar
1 large egg
1 teaspoon vanilla extract
2¼ cups all-purpose flour
1 teaspoon ground cinnamon
¾ teaspoon baking powder
¼ teaspoon salt
3 (1-ounce) squares semisweet chocolate, melted

Beat butter and sugar at medium speed of an electric mixer until fluffy. Add egg and vanilla; beat until blended. Combine flour, cinnamon, baking powder, and salt; add to butter mixture, beating until blended. Add melted chocolate, beating until blended. Cover and chill dough 2 hours.

VANILLA DOUGH

½ cup butter or margarine, softened
½ cup shortening
1 cup sugar
1 large egg
1½ teaspoons vanilla extract
2 cups all-purpose flour
¾ teaspoon baking powder
¼ teaspoon salt

Beat butter and shortening at medium speed of an electric mixer until creamy. Gradually add sugar, beating until light and fluffy. Add egg and vanilla; beat well. Combine flour, baking powder, and salt. Add to butter mixture; beat until blended. Cover and chill dough at least 2 hours.

Variation: If you don't have heart-shaped cookie cutters, use a 2" biscuit cutter; it will give you a larger yield of cookies.

GERMAN CHOCOLATE SLICE 'N' BAKES

Toasted coconut and pecans give these cookies a yummy edge.

1½ cups flaked coconut
1 cup butter, softened
1½ cups sugar
1 (4-ounce) bar sweet baking chocolate, melted and cooled
1 large egg
1 teaspoon vanilla extract
2½ cups all-purpose flour
1 teaspoon baking powder
¼ teaspoon baking soda
⅛ teaspoon salt
1½ cups finely chopped pecans
Milk

Spread coconut in a shallow layer in a 15" x 10" jellyroll pan. Bake at 350° for 13 to 14 minutes or until toasted and dry, stirring once. Cool and transfer coconut to a small zip-top plastic bag. Finely crush coconut, and set aside.

Beat butter at medium speed of an electric mixer until creamy. Gradually add sugar, beating until light and fluffy. Add chocolate; beat well. Add egg and vanilla; beat well.

Combine flour, baking powder, soda, and salt; add to butter mixture, beating until blended. Stir in half of coconut.

Divide dough into thirds; place on 3 large sheets of plastic wrap. Roll each portion lengthwise in plastic wrap, and shape into a 10" log. Cover with plastic wrap, and chill logs 30 minutes. Reroll logs, if necessary.

Combine remaining coconut and pecans. Unwrap logs; brush lightly with milk, and roll in pecan-coconut mixture, pressing firmly to make coating adhere. Wrap in plastic wrap and freeze logs at least 8 hours.

Cut into ¼" slices, using a sharp knife. Place 1" apart on ungreased cookie sheets. Bake at 375° for 8 to 9 minutes or until edges are browned. Cool 1 minute on cookie sheets; remove to wire racks, and cool completely. **Yield:** 7 dozen.

CARAMEL-CASHEW SHORTBREAD BARS

These thick shortbread bars have a crusty, sweet caramel edge. Trim it off if you like. We thought it was yummy.

2 cups all-purpose flour
½ cup sifted powdered sugar
1 cup butter or margarine, cut up
1 (14-ounce) package caramels (we tested with Farley's)
⅓ cup whipping cream
½ cup finely chopped unsalted cashew nuts
¼ cup all-purpose flour
½ cup uncooked regular oats
¼ cup firmly packed brown sugar
¼ cup finely chopped unsalted cashew nuts
⅓ cup butter or margarine, melted

Combine 2 cups flour and powdered sugar in a bowl. Cut 1 cup butter into flour mixture with a pastry blender until mixture is crumbly. Spoon flour mixture into an ungreased 13" x 9" baking dish. Press crumb mixture firmly into pan. Bake at 350° for 20 minutes or until shortbread crust is lightly browned.

Melt caramels and whipping cream in a saucepan over medium heat, stirring frequently. Remove from heat, and stir in ½ cup cashews. Pour over crust in pan.

Combine ¼ cup flour, oats, brown sugar, ¼ cup cashews, and melted butter; stir well. Dollop streusel mixture over caramel in pan, spreading slightly. Bake at 350° for 20 minutes or until edges are lightly browned. Cool completely in pan on a wire rack. Cut into bars, using a sharp knife. **Yield:** 32 bars.

CINNAMON-DATE SHORTBREAD SANDWICHES

Sandwich a sweet date filling between these cinnamon cookies. Use your favorite holiday cookie cutters for variety.

Date Filling
½ cup butter or margarine, softened
⅓ cup sugar
1 cup plus 2 tablespoons all-purpose flour
¾ teaspoon ground cinnamon
½ teaspoon vanilla extract
Powdered sugar (optional)

Prepare Date Filling, and cool completely.
Beat butter at medium speed of an electric mixer until creamy; gradually add sugar, beating until light and fluffy. Add flour, cinnamon, and vanilla, mixing well. Shape dough into a ball. Roll dough to ⅛" thickness on a lightly floured surface; cut with 1½" or 2" round cutters. Use ½" cutter to cut out a star in half of cookies. Pierce solid cookies with a fork or wooden pick.

Place cookies on ungreased cookie sheets. Freeze 10 minutes. Bake at 300° for 20 to 25 minutes or until cookies are very lightly browned. Cool 1 minute on cookie sheet; remove to wire racks, and cool completely.

Spread each solid cookie with about ½ teaspoon of Date Filling. Top each cookie with a cutout cookie, pressing gently to adhere. Sprinkle with powdered sugar, if desired. **Yield:** 2½ dozen.

DATE FILLING

½ (10-ounce) package chopped dates
1 tablespoon sugar
2½ tablespoons water
Pinch of salt

Combine all ingredients in a small saucepan; cook over medium heat, stirring constantly, 3 to 5 minutes or until thickened. Cool completely. **Yield:** ½ cup.

Cinnamon-Date Shortbread Sandwiches

Wheatmeal
Shortbread

WHEATMEAL SHORTBREAD
Pure ingredients blend to make a rich dough that bakes into tender-crisp shortbread.

1 cup butter, softened
¾ cup sifted powdered sugar
2 cups unbleached all-purpose flour
½ cup toasted wheat germ
2 to 3 tablespoons turbinado sugar

Beat butter at medium speed of an electric mixer until creamy; gradually add powdered sugar, beating well. Gradually add flour and wheat germ, beating just until blended. Turn dough out onto wax paper (dough will be soft). Pat dough into a rectangle; cover and chill 30 minutes or until firm.

Transfer dough to a lightly floured work surface; roll to ¼" thickness. Cut dough into 3" x 1" rectangles, using a fluted pastry wheel. Place 1" apart on ungreased cookie sheets. Sprinkle with turbinado sugar.

Bake at 325° for 19 to 20 minutes or until barely golden. Cool 5 minutes on cookie sheets. Remove to wire racks, and cool completely. **Yield:** about 3½ dozen.

Variation: To make shortbread squares, cut dough with fluted-edge square cookie cutters. See page 172 to order cutters.

Turbinado defined: Turbinado sugar is coarse raw sugar with a delicate molasses flavor and golden color. Look for it at large supermarkets near sugar and spices on the baking aisle.

Why unbleached flour? Many gourmet cooks believe flour that hasn't been bleached has the freshest flavor and highest quality for baking. It's the flour to use in simple recipes in which you'll taste the pure flavors. Unbleached and bleached all-purpose flour can be used interchangeably in baking.

135

HAZELNUT TILE BROWNIES

These luscious brownies get a double dose of hazelnut flavor, first from chopped nuts in the crust and then from Frangelico, hazelnut liqueur that you splash into the batter. Rows of milk chocolate squares added after baking resemble rows of tile.

Hazelnut Crust
½ cup butter or margarine
4 (1-ounce) squares semisweet chocolate, fincly chopped
½ cup all-purpose flour
⅛ teaspoon salt
2 large eggs
⅔ cup sugar
1 teaspoon vanilla extract
2 tablespoons Frangelico
16 (⅜-ounce) squares milk chocolate (we tested with Ghirardelli)
Finely chopped hazelnuts, toasted

Prepare Hazelnut Crust; set aside.
Combine butter and semisweet chocolate in a small saucepan; place over medium-low heat. Cook until chocolate and butter melt, stirring until smooth. Cool 10 minutes.
Combine flour and salt; stir well, and set aside.
Combine eggs and sugar in a mixing bowl, and beat at medium-high speed with an electric mixer 3 minutes or until thick and pale. Add cooled chocolate mixture and vanilla; beat well. Add flour mixture, stirring well. Stir in Frangelico.
Pour chocolate batter over crust. Bake at 350° for 32 minutes. (Top will appear cracked.) Place pan on a wire rack. Immediately arrange milk chocolate squares in rows over uncut brownies. Sprinkle with hazelnuts. The heat of the brownies will partially melt the chocolate squares, helping them to "frost" the brownies and hold the nuts on top. Cool and cut into 16 squares. **Yield:** 16 brownies.

HAZELNUT CRUST

1 (2.25-ounce) package chopped hazelnuts, toasted
1 cup all-purpose flour
Pinch of salt
½ cup butter or margarine, cut up and softened
⅓ cup sifted powdered sugar

Line an 8" square pan with aluminum foil; grease foil.
Process hazelnuts, flour, and salt in a food processor 5 seconds or until nuts are finely chopped. Add butter and powdered sugar; pulse until ingredients are combined. Press mixture into pan. Bake at 350° for 12 minutes; cool.
Yield: 1 (8") crust.

DOUBLE CHOCOLATE ESPRESSO BROWNIES

If you love the rich combination of coffee and chocolate, you'll find these brownies irresistible!

Butter-flavored cooking spray
1¼ cups all-purpose flour
¼ teaspoon baking soda
⅛ teaspoon baking powder
⅛ teaspoon salt
14 (1-ounce) squares semisweet chocolate, finely chopped (we tested with Baker's)
1 cup sugar
½ cup butter or margarine
¼ cup light corn syrup
¼ cup espresso or strongly brewed French roast coffee, cooled
3 large eggs
1 tablespoon vanilla extract
1 cup chopped walnuts
6 ounces premium Swiss dark or milk chocolate, coarsely chopped (we tested with Ghirardelli)

Coat a 13" x 9" pan with cooking spray. Line pan with aluminum foil, allowing ends to hang over short sides of pan. Tuck overlapping ends under rim on short sides. Coat foil with cooking spray; set pan aside.
Combine flour and next 3 ingredients in a small bowl. Place chopped semisweet chocolate in a large bowl; set aside.
Combine sugar and next 3 ingredients in a saucepan; cook over medium heat, stirring constantly, until sugar and butter melt and mixture comes to a rolling boil. Remove from heat, and pour over chopped chocolate in bowl; let stand 2 minutes (do not stir).
Beat mixture at low speed of an electric mixer until chocolate melts and mixture is smooth. Add eggs, one at a time, beating well after each addition. Add flour mixture; beat at medium speed until well blended. Stir in vanilla, walnuts, and dark chocolate.
Spoon batter into prepared pan, spreading evenly. Bake at 325° for 45 to 48 minutes. Cool completely in pan on a wire rack. Cover brownies with overlapping foil; chill at least 2 hours.
Carefully invert brownies from pan, using overlapping foil as handles; remove foil. Invert brownies again onto a cutting board; cut into squares or diamonds. **Yield:** 4 dozen.

Double Chocolate
Espresso Brownies

137

PECAN PIE BARS

Pecan pie takes a turn as a bar cookie—and a rich one at that.

2 cups all-purpose flour
½ cup sugar
⅛ teaspoon salt
¾ cup butter or margarine, cut up
1 cup firmly packed brown sugar
1 cup light corn syrup
½ cup butter or margarine
4 large eggs, lightly beaten
2½ cups finely chopped pecans
1 teaspoon vanilla extract

Combine flour, sugar, and salt in large bowl; cut in ¾ cup butter thoroughly with a pastry blender until mixture resembles very fine crumbs. Press mixture evenly into a greased 13" x 9" pan, using a piece of plastic wrap to press crumb mixture firmly in pan. Bake at 350° for 17 to 20 minutes or until lightly browned.

Combine brown sugar, corn syrup, and ½ cup butter in a saucepan; bring to a boil over medium heat, stirring gently. Remove from heat. Stir one-fourth of hot mixture into beaten eggs; add to remaining hot mixture. Stir in pecans and vanilla. Pour filling over crust. Bake at 350° for 34 to 35 minutes or until set. Cool completely in pan on a wire rack. Cut into bars. **Yield:** 16 large bars.

Pecan Pie Bars

Create a Cookie Box

Share the sweet spirit of the season in a beautiful box of cookies. Layer the treats or stack and tie them; then fill your own designer box to offer loved ones.

Organize little stacks of sturdy cookies such as short-bread; tie them with colored raffia, jute, or heavy twine, and nestle them in small decorative boxes like these brown ones with scalloped lids. Trim each container with velvet ribbon. ▼

▲ Purchase a square bakery box from the supermarket, and fill it with an assortment of baked goodies. Add a homemade gift tag for an extra-special touch. We filled the box above with (top, left to right) Two-Tone Cookies, Wheatmeal Shortbread, Hazelnut Tile Brownies, (center) German Chocolate Slice 'n' Bakes, Fudgy Joy Cookies, Chocolate-Apricot Thumbprint Cookies (minus the chocolate), (bottom) Buttercrisp Cookies, Marbled Cinnamon Hearts, and Pecan Pie Bars. How can you get it all done? Bake and freeze cookies up to 3 months in advance.

Give a sturdy white gift box with a cellophane window that hints of homemade sweets inside. Pistachio Brittle or Pecan Pie Bars make a good choice for holiday giving. ▶

SUGAR COOKIE MANTELS

Crown your fireplace with designer cookies. These friendly chocolate critters and sparkling vanilla snowflakes are sure to draw attention from all age groups.

CHOCOLATE MOOSE

Give chocolate sugar cookies as a gift along with a copper moose cookie cutter. Wrap giant cookies in plastic wrap for gift giving, or display them nestled among greenery on your mantel. See page 172 to order the cookie cutter and decorating sugar.

¾ cup butter, softened
1 cup sugar
1 large egg
1 teaspoon vanilla extract
1 cup (6 ounces) semisweet chocolate morsels, melted
2½ cups all-purpose flour
½ teaspoon salt
Sugar
1 (15-ounce) can chocolate frosting
Chocolate sprinkles (optional)
Sparkling white sugar (optional)

Beat butter at medium speed of an electric mixer until creamy; gradually add 1 cup sugar, beating well. Add egg and vanilla, mixing well. Stir in melted morsels.

Combine flour and salt; add to butter mixture, beating well. Shape dough into a flat disc. Cut dough into thirds. Wrap in wax paper. Cover and chill briefly until dough is a good rolling consistency.

Place each portion of dough on a large lightly greased cookie sheet. Cover with wax paper or plastic wrap. Roll dough to ¼" thickness on cookie sheets. Cut out cookies, using desired cookie cutters. (We tested with 3" and 6" moose cutters.) Sprinkle with sugar. Peel away excess dough.

Bake at 350° for 10 to 11 minutes for small cookies and 12 minutes for larger cookies. Cool 5 minutes on cookie sheets; remove to wire racks, and cool completely.

Place opened can of frosting in microwave. Microwave at MEDIUM (50% power) 45 seconds; stir. Microwave 30 more seconds. Spread frosting over cookie antlers and feet, if desired. Sprinkle with chocolate sprinkles and sparkling sugar, if desired. Let harden on wire racks. **Yield**: 9 large cookies or 16 small cookies.

Vanilla Bean Sugar Cookies

Lace these sugar cookies with a double hit of vanilla from the seeds and extract of the vanilla bean. Frost the cookies white, and sprinkle them with iridescent glitter; they'll look like delicate snowflakes. See the variation (below, right) for how to display them on your mantel.

1 vanilla bean
¾ cup butter, softened
¾ cup sugar
1 large egg, lightly beaten
½ teaspoon vanilla extract
2¼ cups all-purpose flour
¼ teaspoon salt
1 (12-ounce) package white chocolate morsels, divided
Shortening
Silver and white edible glitter
Sparkling white sugar

Cut vanilla bean in half lengthwise. Carefully scrape out seeds, using a small sharp knife. Set seeds aside.

Beat butter in a large mixing bowl at medium speed of an electric mixer until creamy. Gradually add sugar and vanilla bean seeds, beating until light and fluffy. Add egg and vanilla extract, mixing well.

Combine flour and salt; gradually add to butter mixture, beating until smooth. Shape dough into four discs. Wrap each in plastic wrap, and chill at least 1 hour.

Roll each disc to ¼" thickness on a lightly floured surface. Cut with 3" and 4" snowflake, star, angel, or Christmas tree cutters. Place on lightly greased cookie sheets. Bake at 350° for 8 to 10 minutes or until edges of cookies are lightly browned. Cool 1 minute on cookie sheets; remove to wire racks, and cool completely.

Combine ½ cup white chocolate morsels and 1 tablespoon shortening in a 1-cup glass measure. Melt morsels according to package directions.

Place cookies on a wire rack over wax paper. Pour or spread white chocolate mixture over each cookie, tilting cookie to coat completely. Sprinkle cookies with glitter and sparkling sugar. Let stand until frosting hardens. Repeat procedure with remaining white morsels, shortening, glitter, and sugar until all cookies are decorated. **Yield:** 3 dozen.

Giant Snowflakes: We used a 6" copper snowflake cookie cutter to yield 1 dozen big cookies that baked 12 minutes. Before baking, we poked holes in each cookie with a drinking straw. Once we decorated and dried them, we wrapped cookies in cellophane bags and tied them with ribbon. We taped each ribbon to the top of the mantel using masking tape, and then covered the tape with white plastic bags and the bags with pots of poinsettias.

CANDY SAMPLER

*Candymaking is one of the season's most enjoyable traditions.
Here is a handful of sweet suggestions for filling your holiday tins.
Watch how quickly the confections disappear.*

Butter-Nut
Truffles

Cookie Dough
Truffles

Eggnog
Truffles

Toffee Truffles

BUTTER-NUT TRUFFLES

You'll recognize a crispy, chocolaty candy bar filling the centers and coating these sinfully rich truffles.

5 (2.1-ounce) chocolate-covered crispy peanut-buttery
   candy bars, frozen (we tested with Butterfinger)
2 (4-ounce) bars bittersweet chocolate, broken into
   pieces (we tested with Ghirardelli)
3 tablespoons whipping cream
3 tablespoons butter or margarine
½ teaspoon butter and nut flavoring

Break 2 candy bars into pieces. Process candy bar pieces in a food processor until finely crushed. Place on a shallow plate, and set aside. Chop remaining 3 candy bars.

Place bittersweet chocolate in food processor bowl, and pulse until finely chopped. Combine whipping cream and butter in a 1-cup glass measure; microwave at HIGH 1 minute or until butter is melted and cream begins to boil. Pour hot cream mixture through food chute with processor running; process until mixture is smooth. Add butter and nut flavoring; process until blended. Transfer mixture to bowl; stir in chopped candy bars. Cover and chill 30 minutes.

Scoop chocolate truffle mixture into 1" balls. Roll in palms of hands to make smooth and uniform balls. Quickly roll in crushed candy bars. Store truffles in refrigerator up to one week. Let stand at room temperature before serving. **Yield:** 2½ dozen.

EGGNOG TRUFFLES

The freezing steps are worth it for the delicious results you get with these truffles. They're better than drinking homemade eggnog.

8 (1-ounce) squares premium white chocolate (we tested
   with Baker's)
½ cup sifted powdered sugar
¼ cup butter, softened
¼ cup refrigerated eggnog
2 tablespoons dark rum
¼ teaspoon ground nutmeg
½ cup finely chopped pecans, toasted
6 ounces vanilla-flavored candy coating

Melt white chocolate in a glass bowl according to package directions. Add powdered sugar, butter, and eggnog; stir gently until mixture is smooth. Add rum and nutmeg, stirring just until blended. Cover and freeze at least 2 hours.

Let truffle mixture stand at room temperature 1 to 2 minutes to soften, if necessary. Using 2 small spoons, shape mixture into 1" balls. Quickly roll in pecans. Place on a wax paper-lined jellyroll pan; cover and freeze until firm.

Melt candy coating according to package directions. Remove truffles from freezer; reshape into balls, if necessary. Using two forks, quickly dip each truffle into melted coating. Place on wax paper to harden. Store truffles in freezer up to one week. **Yield:** 2 dozen.

COOKIE DOUGH TRUFFLES

Here's a new indulgence—chocolate chip cookie dough in candy form, wrapped in a chocolate shell.

½ cup butter, softened
½ cup firmly packed brown sugar
¼ cup sugar
¼ cup thawed egg substitute
1 teaspoon vanilla extract
1¼ cups all-purpose flour
1 cup miniature semisweet chocolate morsels
¾ cup chopped pecans or walnuts
1 (12-ounce) package semisweet chocolate morsels
1½ tablespoons shortening

Beat butter at medium speed of an electric mixer until creamy; gradually add sugars, beating well. Add egg substitute and vanilla; beat well. Add flour to butter mixture; beat well. Stir in miniature chocolate morsels and chopped pecans. Cover and chill 30 minutes.

Shape mixture into 1" balls. Cover and freeze balls until very firm.

Place (12-ounce) package morsels and shortening in a 1-quart glass bowl; melt in microwave according to package directions. Using two forks, quickly dip frozen truffles into melted chocolate, coating completely. Place on wax paper to harden. Store truffles in refrigerator 2 to 3 days. **Yield:** 4½ dozen.

Cookie Dough
Truffles

TOFFEE TRUFFLES

Crushed toffee candy provides a delicious coating for these heavenly chocolate mouthfuls.

8 (1-ounce) squares semisweet chocolate
⅓ cup butter
2 tablespoons whipping cream
¾ cup finely chopped pecans, toasted
4 (1.4-ounce) English toffee-flavored candy bars, crushed
   (see Note)

Heat chocolate squares and butter in a saucepan over medium-low heat, stirring constantly, until melted. Remove from heat; stir in cream. Let cool 5 minutes. Stir in pecans. Cover and chill 2 hours or until mixture is firm.

Shape chocolate mixture into 1" balls; roll in crushed toffee candy. Store truffles in refrigerator up to one week. **Yield:** 2½ dozen.

Note: *Crush toffee bars easily by sealing them in a heavy-duty, zip-top plastic bag; crush with a rolling pin. Use a 1¼" metal scoop to shape the truffles. It streamlines the process.*

PEANUTTY CHOCOLATE NEOPOLITANS

Chocolate, white chocolate, and peanut butter combine in one singular sensation.

Vegetable cooking spray
6 (1-ounce) squares semisweet chocolate, coarsely
   chopped
1 tablespoon creamy peanut butter
8 (1-ounce) squares premium white chocolate, coarsely
   chopped (we tested with Baker's)
2 tablespoons creamy peanut butter
1 (7-ounce) milk chocolate bar, coarsely chopped
   (we tested with Hershey's)
¼ cup chopped unsalted roasted peanuts

Line an 8" square pan with aluminum foil so that it extends at least 2" over sides of pan. Lightly coat pan with cooking spray. Set pan aside.

Combine semisweet chocolate and 1 tablespoon peanut butter in a 1-quart glass bowl. Microwave at HIGH 1 minute. Stir well, and microwave at HIGH 15 seconds to 1 more minute. Stir gently until chocolate melts. Spread chocolate into prepared pan, spreading until smooth with a narrow metal spatula. (Do not clean bowl.) Chill chocolate in pan 15 minutes or just until firm.

Combine white chocolate and 2 tablespoons peanut butter in same bowl. Microwave at HIGH 1 minute. Stir well, and microwave 30 seconds, if necessary. Stir until smooth. Spread white chocolate mixture over first layer in pan, spreading until smooth with a narrow metal spatula. (Do not clean bowl.) Chill pan 15 minutes.

Place milk chocolate in same bowl. Microwave at HIGH 1 to 1½ minutes; stir well. Spread milk chocolate over white chocolate layer. Shake pan to spread evenly. Sprinkle with peanuts. Cover and chill candy 1½ hours or until set.

Score candy into 2" squares. Remove from pan by lifting candy and aluminum foil by foil handles. Cut candy into 2" squares with a long, thin-bladed knife. Place squares on cutting board, and cut each into 4 pieces. **Yield:** 1¼ pounds.

CRUNCHY VANILLA CLUSTERS

A buttery toasted crunch awaits inside these white candy clusters.

1 (3-ounce) package ramen noodles
¾ cup pecan pieces
½ cup sliced almonds
2 tablespoons butter or margarine, melted
1 (12-ounce) package white chocolate or vanilla morsels
   (we tested with Nestlé)

Gently crush ramen noodles before opening package. Open package and discard flavoring packet. Sauté crushed noodles, pecans, and almonds in butter in a large skillet over medium heat until toasted. (Be careful not to crush noodles too finely while sautéing.) Pour noodle mixture into a large bowl to cool.

Melt white chocolate morsels according to package directions. Pour melted chocolate over cooled noodle mixture, tossing gently to coat. Drop candy mixture by rounded tablespoonfuls onto wax paper; let stand until firm (about 45 minutes). Store clusters in an airtight container at room temperature. **Yield:** about 3 dozen.

Note: *It's important to melt white chocolate morsels according to package directions. If heated too quickly or at too high a temperature, the morsels will not melt properly. We recommend using microwave directions for melting.*

Benne Seed Toffee

Crunchy Vanilla Clusters

Peanutty Chocolate Neopolitans

BENNE SEED TOFFEE

The microwave makes this hard candy simple. Light blond in color, the toffee borrows its name, benne, *from the African term for sesame seeds.*

Butter-flavored cooking spray
¾ cup butter
1 cup sugar
3 tablespoons hot water
1 tablespoon light corn syrup
1 (2.38-ounce) jar sesame seeds

Lightly coat a cookie sheet with cooking spray; set aside.
Place butter in a 2-quart microwave-safe bowl. Microwave, covered, at HIGH 1½ to 2 minutes or until butter melts. Stir in sugar, water, and corn syrup. Microwave at HIGH 1 minute. Stir and microwave 3 more minutes. Stir well. Cover and microwave 1 more minute.
Uncover and stir in sesame seeds. Microwave, uncovered, at HIGH 2 to 3 minutes or until candy is light caramel in color. Pour candy onto prepared cookie sheet, spreading to ⅛" thickness. Cool completely on cookie sheet on a wire rack; break candy into pieces. Store in an airtight container. **Yield:** about 1 pound.

PRALINE POPCORN

A brown sugar coating lends this munching corn its rich praline taste.

2 cups pecan halves
¾ cup firmly packed brown sugar
¾ cup maple syrup
½ cup butter
2 teaspoons vanilla extract
1 (3-ounce) bag butter-flavored microwave popcorn, popped (12 cups) (we tested with Orville Redenbacher's Smart Pop)

Place pecans in a large bowl. Set aside.
Combine brown sugar, maple syrup, and butter in a small heavy saucepan; bring to a boil over medium-high heat, stirring often. Reduce heat to medium, and cook 2 minutes, stirring often. Remove from heat, and stir in vanilla.
Drizzle sugar mixture over pecans, tossing to coat. Add popcorn, 2 cups at a time, stirring until well coated.
Spoon popcorn mixture onto a buttered 15" x 10" jelly-roll pan. Bake at 250° for 1 hour, stirring mixture every 15 minutes with a large spoon. Cool completely. Store in an airtight container. **Yield:** 11 cups.

MERRY CHERRY FUDGE

*Chocolate-covered cherries have some new competition. This
easy fudge recipe plants a sweet cherry in every square.*

Vegetable cooking spray
36 maraschino cherries with stems
1 (12-ounce) package semisweet chocolate morsels
6 (1-ounce) squares bittersweet chocolate, chopped
1 (14-ounce) can sweetened condensed milk
1 teaspoon maraschino cherry juice
1 cup chopped pecans

Lightly coat an 8" square pan with cooking spray. Set
aside. Blot cherries dry with paper towels.

Combine chocolates in a heavy saucepan; place over
very low heat, and stir constantly until melted and
smooth. Remove from heat, and stir in sweetened condensed milk and cherry juice. Stir in pecans. Spoon mixture into prepared pan. Immediately press cherries into
fudge, leaving top of each cherry and stem exposed.
Cover and chill fudge 2 hours or until firm.

Cut fudge into 36 squares. Store in an airtight container in refrigerator. **Yield:** 2 pounds.

PISTACHIO BRITTLE

The soft green shade of pistachios perfects a brittle almost too pretty to eat—we said almost.

Butter-flavored cooking spray
1½ cups firmly packed brown sugar
3 tablespoons light corn syrup
2 tablespoons water
1½ tablespoons white vinegar
⅛ teaspoon salt
¼ cup plus 2 tablespoons butter, cut into pieces
1¼ cups shelled pistachio nuts, toasted

Lightly coat a jellyroll pan or large cookie sheet with cooking spray; set aside.

Combine brown sugar and next 4 ingredients in a heavy 2-quart nonstick saucepan. Bring to a boil over medium-high heat, stirring constantly with a wooden spoon. Cover and cook over medium heat 2 to 3 minutes to wash down sugar crystals from sides of pan.

Uncover, and attach a candy thermometer to side of pan. Cook, stirring constantly, until thermometer registers 280°. Add butter.

Cook, stirring constantly, until thermometer registers 300° (hard crack stage). Remove thermometer. Quickly stir in pistachios, immediately pouring mixture onto prepared pan. Quickly press nuts into a single layer within candy mixture. (Candy will not cover pan.) Cool completely; break brittle into pieces. Store in an airtight container. **Yield:** about 1½ pounds.

Pistachio
Brittle

GIFTS & GREETINGS

This season, show your love and appreciation to friends and family with heartfelt tokens that are all handmade.

QUICK GIFTS

Personalize gifts with your own touch to make them more memorable.

◀ PHOTO CARD

Create a handsome tri-paneled card to frame your family's Christmas card photo.

Turn an 8½" x 11" piece of cardstock horizontally and fold the sides inward until they touch. (Use colored cardstock for a richer finish.) When you open the paper you should have three sections.

Using a color copier, copy the patterns from pages 170-171, and cut them apart. Center the frame on the large middle area inside the card, and glue along the top edge only. Center the two long rectangular illustrations on the inside side panels, and glue along all sides. Trim the top and bottom edges of the cardstock, if desired.

Close the card, and place the triangles on either side of the opening to form a diamond shape. Glue in place.

Referring to the photograph at left for position, use a paper hole punch to make two holes on the front of the card. Slide a 3½" x 5" photo in place behind the frame, gluing to hold in place if desired. Thread ribbon or cording through the holes, tie to close.

GIFT CARDS ▲

Delight friends with an elegant card that, with an attached decorative pin, becomes a gift.

From handmade paper, cut out a rectangle, and fold it in half to make a card. Adhere rectangles of coordinating colors of other handmade papers to the front of the card, layering smaller pieces on top of bigger ones. Stick the pin to the center of the card, penetrating through all layers. Even when the pin is removed, an attractive card remains.

▲ **DECORATED DISH** Jazz up a plain white platter for a terrific hostess gift. (Check restaurant-supply stores for great prices on plates.) Use a hot-glue gun to attach an assortment of greenery, flowers, berries, and ribbons to the plate. You may consider making a set of matching plates to hang on the wall or trimming small saucers to use as jewelry dishes.

PAINTED NAPKINS

Add a little holiday whimsy to plain paper napkins. Using a paint pen, write a favorite verse or words to a carol around the edge of the napkin. Draw a design in the center of the napkin, if desired. Tie a stack of napkins together with a fancy ribbon to make a gift.

For a classic look, use silver and gold paint pens. For a playful look, use red and green pens. For designs, draw stars or trees—anything that's easy and fast. After all, these are napkins that can be thrown away!

BEADED TOPPERS ▶

Here's a variation on the bottle topper theme using beads instead of finials.

Drill a small hole in a cork, being careful not to go all the way through. Choose a drill bit to suit the size of the copper wire you will use to thread the beads. Put a drop of heavy-duty glue in the hole, and insert the wire into the hole. (Be sure the wire will fit through the holes in your beads.) After the glue dries, slide on a flat bead and then coil the wire, using pliers to bend the wire, if necessary. Thread additional beads on the wire. Cut the wire about ³⁄₈" above the last bead. To finish, put a drop of glue just above the last bead, attach the end of a length of gold craft wire, and wrap the gold wire tightly around the end of the copper wire. When removing the topper from the bottle, grasp the cork—not the beads.

◀ FINIAL TOPPERS

Present one of these fancy, handmade bottle toppers to your favorite wine lover. Paint an unfinished wooden drapery finial with metallic paint. When the paint has dried, put a drop of glue on the top of a cork, and screw the finial into the cork securely. When using the topper, be sure to grasp the cork—not the finial— to pull the topper from the bottle.

SNUGGLY HAT AND GLOVES Create a stylish gift ensemble when you embellish a hat and a pair of gloves with silk roses and ribbon. Using simple stitches, tack a ribbon around the hat to form a band, and add a ribbon rose to the hatband and glove cuffs. To make ribbon roses, see page 166. For the leaves, fold a short piece of ribbon, and tack it in place.

COZY FLEECE THROW

With this warm greeting, you'll be remembered fondly all winter long.

Purchase an inexpensive fleece throw. For the snowflake motifs, we used ½ yard of teal felt, ¼ yard of white felt, and 1 yard of paper-backed fusible web.

From the teal felt, cut 5 (9") squares. Using the patterns on page 168, trace 3 from "Snowflake A" and 2 from "Snowflake B" onto the paper-backed fusible web. Fuse all 5 snowflakes to the white felt. Cut out along the drawn lines, and remove the paper backing.

Center one snowflake on each of the 5 teal squares.

Cover the snowflakes with a press cloth, and fuse them to the teal squares.

Cut 10 (½" x 9") strips from the paper-backed fusible web. On the wrong side of each teal square, fuse 2 strips of paper-backed fusible web to the outer edges. Remove the paper backing. Arrange the teal squares along one edge of the fleece blanket. Make sure they are evenly spaced from the bottom edge of the blanket. (The ones pictured are spaced 3¼" apart and 3¼" above the bottom edge of the blanket.) Cover the squares with a press cloth, and fuse them to the blanket. Hand washing is recommended for the throw.

GIFT GIVING MADE SIMPLE Examples of three treasured holiday collections are shown here. This season, start one for someone you love or even yourself. It gives family and friends an idea of what to give you each year, and it's just plain fun to collect and display all of the different pieces. The collection becomes a family heirloom, and everyone will enjoy admiring it from year to year. Be sure to take a photo of how it is set up and save yourself time next Christmas.

Winter
Wonderland
Village

Soft Stuffed
Santas

Shell Angel
Ornaments

WONDERFUL WRAPPINGS

Packages gloriously adorned with ribbons, bows, and fancy trimmings enhance the magical anticipation of the grand opening.

SPECIAL TAGS AND TRIMS

Gift packages creatively wrapped with ingenious toppers and tags make the presentation almost as much fun as the gift itself.

WIRED STARS Bring a stellar dimension to your package with metallic stars. Take two star stickers, put a thin wire between them, and press together. Attach the other end of the wire to the ribbon wrapped around the present. These embellishments are especially striking when combined with star-design wrapping paper. For variety, use different sizes and colors of stickers.

VELLUM TAGS ▲

These artful gift tags take only moments to make. Cut a tag from vellum, and layer it on a slightly larger tag cut from solid-colored paper. Using a paper hole punch, make a hole through both tags. Tie ribbon or cording through them, and attach to the package. Write your message on the vellum with a paint pen. For an extra touch, use a star hole punch, and make a hole in the vellum so the background color shows through.

PACKAGE PANACHE

Elevate a stick-on bow to star status by tying a small ornament, candy cane, charm, or tassel to one of the bow's loops. Or pair the bow with additional ribbons wrapped around the box. It's an easy way to give your gifts a little extra style.

WIRE TAGS ▼

Give your gifts distinction by adding a wire star or squiggle to the tag. Use needle-nose pliers to twist solder wire into various shapes. Bring a little color into the tag by sliding a bead on one end of the wire. Use these wire creations to embellish a napkin holder, give as a party favor, or attach as a package topper.

STAR TAG ▶

For a quick and easy tag, copy the star-shaped tag on page 170 on a color copier. Enlarge or shrink the tag to fit the size of the present. If you don't have access to a color copier, trace the pattern on white paper, and color stripes along the edges with a red marker.

◀ HEXAGONAL TAG

Trace or photocopy the hexagonal tag on page 170. For a clever switch from ribbon, wrap coordinating rickrack around a box, and glue the gift tag to the top of the present, securing the ends of the rickrack underneath the tag.

Papier-mâché boxes, like the one shown here, come in all shapes and sizes at crafts and discount stores. They're good for gift boxes and sturdy enough to use later for storage or decoration.

SNOWMAN TAG ▶

Trace or photocopy the snowman tag on page 170. Enlarge or shrink it to fit the gift container. Wrap rickrack around the present and attach the gift tag to the top, securing the ends of the rickrack under the tag.

This circular tag is perfectly designed to fit on a papier-mâché cylinder, which makes a good container for cookies or other homemade treats.

PINWHEEL TOPPER Delight children of all ages with a pinwheel gift topper. Trace the pattern on page 170 onto two different colored pieces of paper. Adhere the wrong sides of the papers together, and cut on the designated lines. Punch a small hole in the center of the pentagon and in the left corner of each triangle that's created. Stick a pipe cleaner through the back of the pentagon, bringing it through the front. Fold each of the triangles toward the center, and slide the pipe cleaner through each of the holes to create a pinwheel. Loop the end of the pipe cleaner through the back of a jingle bell, and twist so it lays flat on the pinwheel. Attach the pinwheel to a candy cane, and slide the candy stick through the knot of a bow to hold it in place.

▲ **BEAD BOWS** Use beads instead of ribbons to make bows for your most special packages. String beads on thin wire, and twist to make loops. Attach the loops to each other with wire and then to the ribbon on the package. Gift wrap as pretty as this should definitely qualify as part of the gift! Fill a bowl with these beaded boxes for a festive centerpiece or table decoration.

FANCY FABRIC WRAPS ▲

For a luxurious-looking package, wrap gifts with remnants of decorator fabric. Place a box in the center of a square piece of fabric with the box's corners positioned at right angles to the fabric's corners. Fold one corner of fabric over the top of the box, followed by the opposite corner. Tie the other two corners in a knot over the center of the box. Hot-glue trim to the edges for a neat finish.

To wrap a cylinder, place the container at the corner edge of a square piece of fabric and roll it up. Tie the remaining fabric ends into tight knots. Tuck in loose ends and secure at the base of the knot with ribbon, hiding raw edges. Hot-glue ribbon to the fabric to hide raw edges.

VELVET BUNDLES ▶

Give a small gift a big presentation by delivering it in a soft, velvet purse. Cut a circle of velvet and glue cording along the edges. Place the gift in the center of the fabric, and wrap the sides up around it. Gather the excess fabric to create a pouch, and tie it closed with decorative cording. Add an ornament to embellish the knot, if desired.

PATTERNS

FRONT DOOR TREE (PAGE 37)
Base Assembly

1. To make the tree's base, cut a 1" sheet of Styrofoam at an angle 19" from the middle center down each side *(Diagram 1)*. Place the two remaining triangles on each side of the main piece to form the tree *(Diagram 2)*. Use hot glue and florist picks to hold the pieces together.

2. Measure 28" down from the top of the tree. Trim the remaining Styrofoam across the bottom of the tree. From the remaining Styrofoam, cut a piece the same size as the papier-mâché pot. Hot-glue the Styrofoam piece to the back of the pot. Use hot glue and florist picks to attach the pot to the tree.

19" 19"

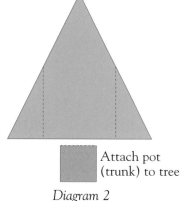

Attach pot (trunk) to tree

Diagram 1   *Diagram 2*

JINGLE BELL DOOR CHIME (PAGE 40)

1. Cut approximately 4 (14"-18") lengths of cording (wired cording works best). Knot one large jingle bell to each end of each length of cording *(Diagram 1)*.

2. Loop each length, grouping them together between your thumb and index finger. Form the bells into a grape-like cluster by gently pulling each bell into position.

3. When the bells are in the desired position, secure the loops by wrapping them tightly with a length of cording or craft wire *(Diagram 2)*.

4. For the hanger, tie ribbon through the loop opening at the top of the cluster.

Diagram 1

Diagram 2

STAMPED WITH STYLE (PAGE 40)
Mailbox Arrangement Assembly

1. Cover a florist foam block with sheet moss. Wrap chicken wire around the foam block, overlapping the wire and securing it to itself with plastic-coated wire *(Photo 1)*. Fold up the chicken wire at the ends of the block and wire in place. Repeat the same procedure with another block of foam. Soak the blocks in water until they are thoroughly wet.

2. Using a length of plastic-coated wire, fasten the blocks together at each of the long sides. Leave enough wire between the blocks to go over the top of the mailbox and to allow the blocks to rest on each side of the mailbox.

3. Insert greenery into the florist foam, as desired, until the forms are no longer visible *(Photo 2)*. Work from side to side to keep the weight balanced across the mailbox. Use florist picks and wire to attach heavy materials and to attach the bow. Wet the foam blocks every few days to keep the greenery fresh.

SNUGGLY HAT AND GLOVES (PAGE 154)

For each ribbon rose, working ¼" from the edge, run gathering stitches down the right edge and along the bottom edge of the ribbon *(Diagram 1)*. Pull the thread to gather tightly *(Diagram 2)*. Roll gathered ribbon into a rosette, tacking along bottom edge to secure *(Diagram 3)*.

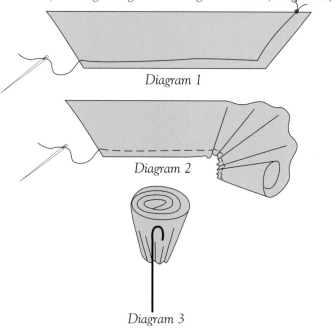

Diagram 1

Diagram 2

Diagram 3

STARRY NIGHT PLACE MATS (PAGE 69)
Patterns are full-size.

Large Tree

Medium Tree

Small Tree

Star

SNOWFLAKE TABLE RUNNER (PAGE 69)
Patterns are full-size.

Place on fold of paper.

Place on fold of paper.

SNOWFLAKE TAGS* (PAGE 95)

Patterns are full-size.

Place on fold of paper.

Place on fold of paper.

Place on fold of paper.

Place on fold of paper.

SNOWFLAKE PLACE CARDS* (PAGE 95)

Pattern is full-size.

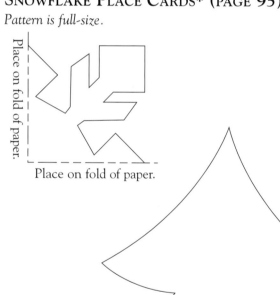

Place on fold of paper.

Place on fold of paper.

COZY FLEECE THROW* (PAGE 155)

Patterns are full-size.

Place on fold of paper.

Place on fold of paper.

Snowflake A

Snowflake B

Place on fold of paper.

Place on fold of paper.

TREE TREE SKIRT
(PAGE 107)

Pattern is full-size.

*HOW TO FOLD PAPER TO MAKE SNOWFLAKE PATTERNS

Fold paper in half.

Fold in half again.

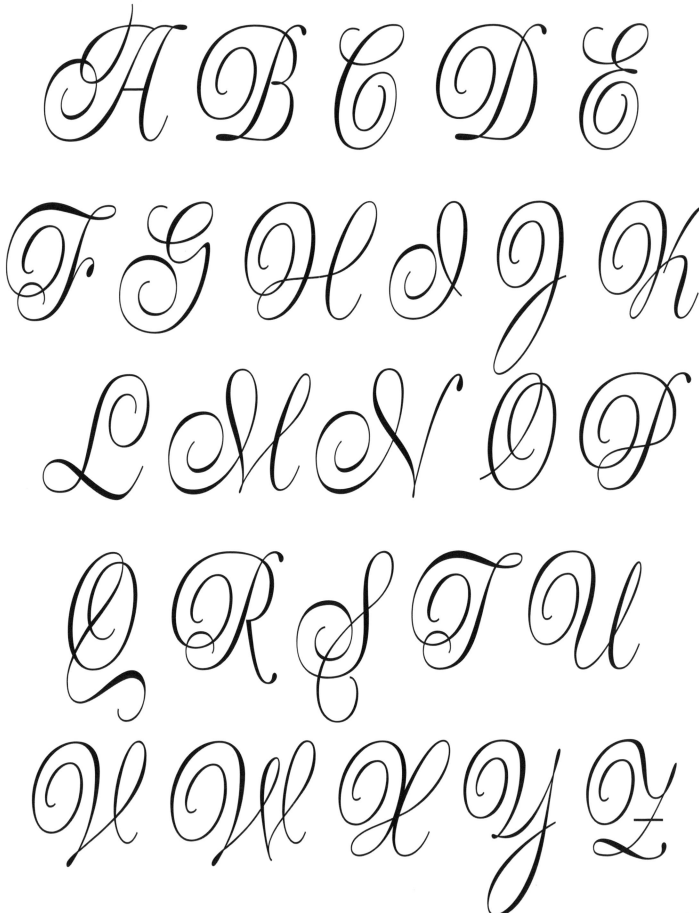

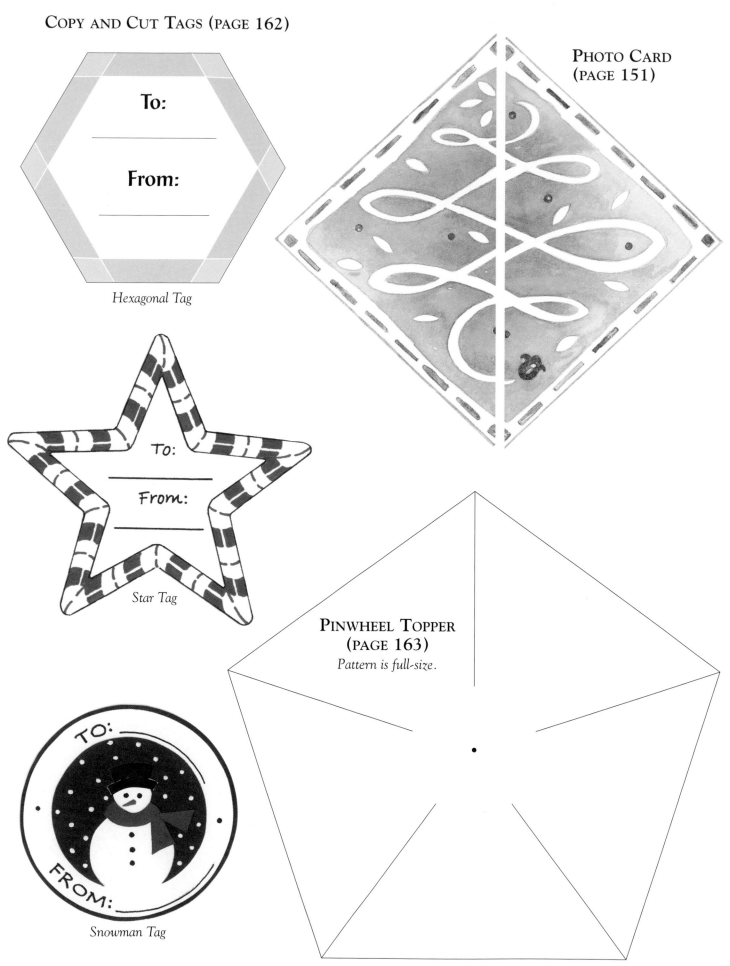

COPY AND CUT TAGS (PAGE 162)

Hexagonal Tag

PHOTO CARD
(PAGE 151)

Star Tag

PINWHEEL TOPPER
(PAGE 163)
Pattern is full-size.

TO:

FROM:

Snowman Tag

PHOTO CARD
(PAGE 151)

Cut out center of card
along inside green line.

WHERE TO FIND IT

Source information is current at time of publication.

Artificial greenery garlands and wreaths: To find a Michaels Arts and Crafts Store nearest you, call (800) 642-4235.

Beads: Contact Beadbox Inc., 1290 N. Scottsdale Rd., Tempe, AZ 85281, or at www.beadbox.com.

Candy and confections: Contact Hammond Candy Company, 4969 Colorado Blvd., Denver, CO 80216, or call (888) CANDY-99.

Fresh greenery garlands and wreaths: Contact Laurel Springs Christmas Tree Farm, LLC, Hwy 18 South, P.O. Box 85, Laurel Springs, NC 28644, or call (800) 851-2345.

Styrofoam forms: To find a Michaels Arts and Crafts Store nearest you, call (800) 642-4235.

Pages 8-12—artificial greenery, fruit, and dried materials: To find a Michaels Arts and Crafts Store nearest you, call (800) 642-4235.

Page 8-12—florist foam form: To find a Michaels Arts and Crafts Store nearest you, call (800) 642-4235.

Pages 8-12—ribbon: Contact Vaban Gille, Inc., P.O. Box 420747, San Francisco, CA 94142, or call (417) 552-5490.

Page 17—copper garden labels used as place cards: Contact Smith and Hawken, 117 E. Strawberry Drive, Mill Valley, CA 94941, or call (800) 776-5558.

Page 19—applewood smoked bacon: Contact Nueske's at (800) 392-2266, or at www.nueske.com.

Page 25—flatware: Contact Table Matters, 2409 Montevallo Road, Birmingham, AL 35223, or call (205) 879-0125.

Page 25—pewter bowl and plate: Contact Old World Pewter, P.O. Box 245, Clermont, GA 30527, or call (770) 983-7030.

page 26

Pages 26-27—table decorations: Contact Henhouse Antiques, 1900 Cahaba Road, Birmingham, AL 35223, or call (205) 918-0505.

Pages 28-29—ribbon: Contact C.M. Offray & Son, Inc., 360 Rt. 24, Chester, NJ 07930-0601.

Pages 46-47—candles: Contact Ana Design, 1 Ott Street, Trenton, NJ 08638, or call (609) 394-0300.

Pages 46-47—florist foam wreath: Contact Galveston Wreath Company, 1124 25th Street, Galveston, TX 77550-4409, or call (800) 874-8597.

Page 57—candle adapter: To find a Michaels Arts and Crafts Store nearest you, call (800) 642-4235.

Page 60—stockings: Contact Pottery Barn at (800) 922-5507.

Pages 68-69—felt: Contact Kunin Felt, P.O. Box 5000, Hampton, NH 03843, or at www.kuninfelt.com.

Page 69—place mat: To find a Michaels Arts and Crafts Store nearest you, call (800) 642-4235.

Pages 72-73— antique lavender and white china pieces: Contact Bridges Antiques, 3949 Cypress Drive, Birmingham, AL 35243, or call (205) 967-6233.

Pages 72-73—antique tiered piece: Contact The Chinaberry, 1 Hoyt Lane, Birmingham, AL 35213, or call (205) 879-5338.

Pages 72-73—champagne ice bucket: Contact Bridges Antiques, 3949 Cypress Drive, Birmingham, AL 35243, or call (205) 967-6233.

Pages 72-73—glass container: Contact Christine's, 2822 Petticoat Lane, Birmingham, AL 35223, or call (205) 871-8297.

Page 74— antique plate: Contact Bridges Antiques, 3949 Cypress Drive, Birmingham, AL 35243, or call (205) 967-6233.

Page 78—tray: Contact Christine's, 2822 Petticoat Lane, Birmingham, AL 35223, or call (205) 871-8297.

Pages 80-81—colored glass plates: Contact Table Matters, 2409 Montevallo Road, Birmingham, AL 35223, or call (205) 879-0125.

Pages 80-81—gold and copper glass bowls: Contact Annieglass, 310 Harvest Drive, Watsonville, CA 95076, or call (800) 347-6133.

Page 82—tray: Contact Mariposa, 5 Elm Street, Manchester, MA 01944, or call (978) 526-9944.

Page 83—ribbon: Contact Midori, Inc., 708 6th Ave. North, Seattle, WA 98199, or call (206) 282-3595.

Page 83—barquette molds: Contact Williams-Sonoma, 3250 Van Ness Ave., San Francisco, CA 94109, or at www.williams-sonoma.com.

Page 83—tray: Contact Christine's, 2822 Petticoat Lane, Birmingham, AL 35223, or call (205) 871-8297.

Page 86—chair scarf: Contact Crate & Barrel, 725 Landwehr Road, Northbrook, IL 60062, or call (800) 451-8217.

Page 91—napkin decorations: To find a Michaels Arts and Crafts Store nearest you, call (800) 642-4235.

Page 95—holographic paper: To find a Michaels Arts and Crafts Store nearest you, call (800) 642-4235.

Page 96—china: Contact The China Closet, 634 Montgomery Highway, Vestavia Hills, AL 35216, or call (205) 822-6499.

Page 97—linens: Contact Pintucks and Pinafores, 4300 Paces Ferry Road, Suite 405, Atlanta, GA 30339, or call (888) 342-6478.

Page 112—napkin: Contact Table Matters, 2409 Montevallo Road, Birmingham, AL 35223, or call (205) 879-0125.

Page 112—plate: Contact Eigen Arts, 150 Bay Street 9th Floor, Jersey City, NJ 07302, or call (201) 798-7310.

Page 113—plate: Contact Table Matters, 2409 Montevallo Road, Birmingham, AL 35223, or call (205) 879-0125.

Page 117—napkins and place mats: Contact Karavan, 20 Jones Street, New Rochelle, NY 10801, or call (914) 654-0300.

Page 117—plates: Contact Pastis and Company, 300 East 54th Street - 14E, New York, NY 10022, or call (212) 838-0776.

Page 117—rosemary wreath plants: Contact Plant Odyssey, 2912 6th Ave. South, Birmingham, AL 35233, or call (205) 324-0566.

Page 118—plates: Contact Pastis and Company, 300 East 54th Street - 14E, New York, NY 10022, or call (212) 838-0776.

Page 119—trifle bowl: Contact Williams-Sonoma, 3250 Van Ness Ave., San Francisco, CA 94109, or at www.williams-sonoma.com.

Page 119—velvet ribbons: Contact MKB Ribbons, 561 7th Ave., 11th Floor, New York, NY 10018, or call (212) 302-5010.

Page 120—antique French buffet: Contact French Market Antiques Warehouse, 204 West Coosa Street, Talladega, AL 35160, or call (256) 362-4700.

Page 120-123—monogrammed napkins, platter, plates: Contact Christine's, 2822 Petticoat Lane, Birmingham, AL 35223, or call (205) 871-8297.

Page 124— antique pewter coffee pot and cups: Contact The Chinaberry, 1 Hoyt Lane, Birmingham, AL 35213, or call (205) 879-5338.

Page 128—ribbon: Contact Vaban Gille, P.O. Box 420747, San Francisco, CA 94142, or call (417) 552-5490.

Page 130—antique silver tray: Contact Bridges Antiques, 3949 Cypress Drive, Birmingham, AL 35243, or call (205) 967-6233.

Page 131—cherub statuary: Contact CAST ART, 1713 2nd Ave. South, Birmingham, AL 35233, or call (205) 324-3936.

Page 131—cup: Contact Marge Margulies Pottery, 6801 Sprague Street, Philadelphia, PA 19119, or call (215) 844-9603.

Page 131—wire mesh cones: Contact SNK Enterprises, Inc., P.O. Box 6702, Chesterfield, MO 63006, or call (314) 991-8570.

Page 132—red burlap gift bags: RAH, 1413 23rd Street, Galveston, TX 77550, or call (409) 621-4652.

Page 134—Edme cup and saucer: Contact Waterford Wedgwood, 1330 Campus Parkway, Wall, NJ 07719, or call (732) 938-5800.

Page 134—snowman ornament: Contact Christmas and Company at (205) 943-0020.

Page 134—striped cookie jar: Ronnie Ceramics, 5999 3rd Street, San Francisco, CA 94124, or call (800) 888-8218.

Page 135—fluted cookie cutters: Contact Bridge Kitchenware at (800) 274-3435, or at www.bridgekitchenware.com.

Page 135—red ribbon: Contact Vaban Gille, P.O. Box 420747, San Francisco, CA 94142, or call (417) 552-5490.

Pages 137-138—glass cake pedestal, covered etched cake pedestal: Contact Christine's, 2822 Petticoat Lane, Birmingham, AL 35223, or call (205) 871-8297.

Page 138—plate: Contact Annieglass, 310 Harvest Drive, Watsonville, CA 95076, or call (800) 347-6133.

Page 138—ribbon: Contact Vaban Gille, P.O. Box 420747, San Francisco, CA 94142, or call (417) 552-5490.

Page 139—colored raffia: To find a Michaels Arts and Crafts Store nearest you, call (800) 642-4235.

Page 139—scalloped brown boxes: To find a Michaels Arts and Crafts Store nearest you, call (800) 642-4235.

Page 139—velvet/satin ribbon: Contact Midori Ribbon, Inc., 708 6th Ave. North, Seattle WA 98109, or call (206) 282-3595.

Page 140—copper moose cookie cutter: Contact Sur La Table, 1765 6th Ave. South, Seattle, WA 98134, or call (800) 243-0852, or at www.surlatable.com.

Pages 140-141—edible glitter, sparkling white sugar: Contact the The Baker's Catalogue, P.O. Box 876, Norwich, VT 05055, or call (800) 827-6836, or at www.kingarthurflour.com.

Page 141—copper snowflake cookie cutter: Contact Williams-Sonoma, 3250 Van Ness Ave., San Francisco, CA 94109, or at www.williams-sonoma.com.

Page 145—red glasses: Contact Studio Sgobbare, 103 Webster Street Unit 1, Pawtucket, RI 02861, or call (401) 722-4550.

Page 151—handmade paper, Page 161—vellum: To find a Michaels Arts and Crafts Store nearest you, call (800) 642-4235.

Page 162—papier-mâché boxes: To find a Michaels Arts and Crafts Store nearest you, call (800) 642-4235.

General Index

page 161

RECIPE INDEX

Gingerbread Trifle, page 119

Endive Salad with Pancetta, page 120

CONTRIBUTORS

Editorial Contributors:
Barbara Ashford
Lowell Baltzell
Peggy Barnhart
Melanie J. Clarke
Adrienne Davis
Betty Drennen
Liz Edge
Connie Formby
Judy Hill
Margot Hotchkiss
Susan Huff
Lorrie Hulston
Ray Jordan
Amy Kendrick
Duffy Morrison
Cecile Nierodzinski
Catherine Pewitt
Alison and James Scotney
Betsy Cooper Scott
Elizabeth Taliaferro
Dinah Toro
Cynthia Moody Wheeler
Contributing Photographers:
Jean Allsopp
Van Chaplin
Emily Minton
Thanks to the following homeowners:
Pam and Tom Buck
Kay and Eddie Clarke
Judy and Rusty Fuller
Julie and Barry Gunter
Cathy and Sam Harris
Lynn and Chip Hazelrig
Susan and Don Huff
Beth and Jimmy Jordan
Cathy and Roger Lee
Georgine and Lawrence Lemak
Karen and Todd Pegram
Barbara and Ed Randle
Jeanne and Mabry Rodgers
Karen and Harold Stephens
Jackie and Fred Wedell
Olivia and Jack Wells
Madeline and Bill White
Robin and Mike Wood
Linda and Kneeland Wright
Thanks to the following businesses:
China Closet
Henhouse Antiques
Martin and Son Wholesale Florist
Paper Works Outlet

HOLIDAY PLANNING GUIDE

Embrace the season with zealous glee with the help of this handy guide. You'll find spacious calendars, tidy list boxes, and useful tips— all in one place. With this special section, you're on your way to the most organized, most carefree Christmas ever.

November 2000

Use this handy calendar to list all the things you have to do (and want to do!)
during this month that sets the stage for the fun holidays to come.

Sunday	Monday	Tuesday	Wednesday
			1
5	6	7	8
12	13	14	15
19	20	21	22
26	27	28	29

Thursday	Friday	Saturday	*Things to Do:*
2	3	4	
9	10	11	
16	17	18	
Thanksgiving 23	24	25	
30			

December 2000

Free yourself from tiny notes that are scattered from the refrigerator door to the bottom of your purse. Write all of your errands on this calendar, and you'll be set for a stress-free holiday.

Sunday	Monday	Tuesday	Wednesday
3	4	5	6
10	11	12	13
17	18	19	20
Christmas Eve 24			
31	Christmas 25	26	27

Thursday	Friday	Saturday	Things to Do:
	1	2	
7	8	9	
14	15	16	
21	22	23	
28	29	30	

Helpful Holiday Hints

These tips answer some of the season's basic decorating and cooking questions, leaving you more time to sit back with a warm mug of cocoa and enjoy the holidays.

TIPS FOR FRESH DECORATING

•Group pots of fragrant paperwhites, amaryllis, cyclamen, or poinsettias together on the mantel, hearth, or tabletop for a more dramatic display than a single plant would give.

•When using natural decorations indoors, put them up no sooner than two weeks before Christmas (or your special event). Misting the decorations with water will help foil the effects of indoor heat.

•Look to your cupboard for decorative containers to fill with natural materials gathered from your backyard. Wooden salad bowls, wire baskets, and pitchers filled with pinecones, holly, nandina, and magnolia leaves make instant mantel and tabletop arrangements.

GREENERY & FLOWER FAVORITES

Accent greenery clipped from your backyard with a few fresh blooms from the florist. Some fresh materials to consider are holly and berries, nandina greenery and berries, magnolia leaves, ivy, pine and cedar cuttings, red and white carnations, roses, and lilies. List your favorites here for quick reference.

DECORATING IDEAS

Use this list to note ideas you want to repeat next year, including numbers used (such as strings of lights, number of garlands, etc.) and how the decorations were installed.

POINSETTIA POINTERS

•Choose a poinsettia that has dark green foliage all the way down the stem. Bracts (the leaves that turn color) should not have a green cast.

•The set of buds in the center of the plant should be small and tightly clustered. Buds that are withered or have fallen off signify a plant that is past its prime.

•Poinsettias need bright but not direct sunlight, at least six hours a day. Water plants with lukewarm (never cold) water, keeping soil moist. Overwatering may cause the leaves to drop.

WINE TIPS & TIDBITS

•Don't cook with a wine you wouldn't drink.

•When recipes call for a small amount of wine, small bottles—called splits—are the best buy.

•Store open bottles of wine corked and refrigerated up to one week.

•Don't throw out leftover wine. Freeze it in ice trays and store in zip-top plastic bags for use in soups, stews, sauces, and casseroles.

•Substitute broth or fruit juice for wine in some recipes, but you may lose the full-bodied flavor of the dish.

LAST-MINUTE ENTERTAINING

If you're short on time during the holidays, here's a list of items you can pick up at the market and have on hand for unexpected guests. No recipes needed.

•Jar of olives (black, green, or Greek kalamata)
•Grissini (skinny breadsticks)
•Herb-flavored cheese
•8-ounce package cream cheese; top with your favorite preserves or jelly (we recommend fig preserves, jalapeño jelly, or mint jelly). Serve with specialty crackers.
•Tub of fruited cream cheese; serve with gingersnaps and seasonal fruit.
•Jar of lemon curd; serve with store-bought pound cake or angel food cake.
•An assortment of flavored tea bags, flavored coffee, hot cocoa and mini marshmallows

ALCOHOL SUBSTITUTION CHART
Here's a handy list of substitutions if you prefer your recipes to be nonalcoholic.

If The Recipe Calls For:	Substitute:
2 tablespoons Grand Marnier or other orange-flavored liqueur	2 tablespoons orange juice and ½ teaspoon orange extract or 2 tablespoons unsweetened orange juice concentrate
2 tablespoons rum or brandy	½ to 1 teaspoon rum or brandy extract or 2 tablespoons water, white grape juice, or apple juice
2 tablespoons amaretto or other almond-flavored liqueur	¼ to ½ teaspoon almond extract
2 tablespoons bourbon	1 to 2 teaspoons vanilla extract
2 tablespoons sherry	1 to 2 teaspoons vanilla extract or 2 tablespoons orange or pineapple juice
2 tablespoons Kahlúa or other coffee- or chocolate-flavored liqueur	½ to 1 teaspoon chocolate extract plus ½ to 1 teaspoon instant coffee granules dissolved in 2 tablespoons hot water
¼ cup or more port, sweet sherry, rum, brandy, liqueur	Equal measure of unsweetened orange juice or apple juice plus 1 teaspoon of corresponding flavored extract or vanilla extract
¼ cup or more white wine	Equal measure of white grape juice, chicken broth, vegetable broth, clam juice, or nonalcoholic wine. If you use nonalcoholic wine, add a tablespoon of vinegar to cut the sweetness.
¼ cup or more red wine	Equal measure of red grape juice, cranberry juice, apple cider, chicken broth, beef broth, vegetable broth, clam juice, flavored vinegar, or nonalcoholic wine. If you use nonalcoholic wine, add a tablespoon of vinegar to cut the sweetness.

Note: *Add water, white grape juice, apple juice, or broth, if necessary, to get the specified amount of liquid called for in the recipe.*

Entertaining Planner

We entertain to have a good time and, especially during the holidays, to create wonderful memories.
Use the lines on these pages to organize your plans for the most memorable parties of the year.

GUEST LIST

Use these lines to make a list of the guests you want to invite to each of your holiday gatherings.
Make it easy on yourself and include phone numbers alongside the names.

Menu

Add a new showstopping dish to this year's
food lineup. It's a great conversation starter.

SET A SIMPLE BUFFET

• To save time, take advantage of precut vegetables and fruits at the supermarket.

• Consider buying ready-to-eat dips for your vegetable buffet and chocolate or caramel sauce for the fruit/dessert buffet.

• Estimate three drinks, three glasses, and three napkins for each guest for a two-hour party.

• Supply each end of the buffet table with more than enough napkins and utensils for all guests.

LAST-MINUTE DETAILS

Get a jump on last-minute party tasks by listing them here.

PARTY SUPPLIES LIST

From napkins to ice to flowers, you'll remember all the party supplies easily when you write them down before-hand on the lines offered below.

PARTY TO-DO LIST

Check for guest towels, press tablecloths, light candles— it's easy to remember every detail when you've written it down on a checklist.

185

Christmas Dinner Planner

The Christmas feast is more an event than a meal. And since every event is made easier with planning, use these pages to write down all the important details for this holiday tradition.

GUEST LIST

....
....
....
....
....
....
....
....
....
....
....
....
....
....
....
....
....
....
....
....
....
....

DINNER TO-DO LIST

This list can include everything from buying the food to setting the table.

....
....
....
....
....
....
....
....
....
....
....
....
....
....

THAWING THE TURKEY

An 8- to 12-pound turkey takes one to two days to thaw in the refrigerator. If you've forgotten that part and it's too late, leave the turkey in its unopened bag and place it in a large container of cold water. Change the water every 30 minutes for 6 hours or until the turkey thaws.

Menu

PARTY NOTES

Would you do something differently for next year's dinner? Was there a particularly favorite dish on the menu? Record it here so you'll remember it next Christmas.

....
....
....
....
....
....
....
....
....
....
....
....
....
....
....

CRAFTY CENTERPIECES

• Build a sideboard decoration around favorite pieces of pottery. Mugs and pitchers can serve as vases for slim evergreen branches and stems of berries, while bowls can be filled with polished pomegranates, apples, or pears. Propping a large plate or platter against the wall behind the arrangement adds a unifying background.

• For the kitchen, copper and brass cookware sets a mellow mood for a tabletop grouping. Fill a chafing dish or colander with bundles of cinnamon sticks and bittersweet berries. Copper cookie cutters, candy molds, even measuring cups and spoons are nice additions to this innovative approach.

• Arrange your favorite pieces of glassware, such as drinking glasses, vases, and pitchers. Fill the containers with brightly colored Christmas candies—both small, round pieces and tall candy sticks and canes. Place glass candleholders among the glasses to illuminate the setting.

• Fill a clear glass vase with delicate greenery clippings such as wispy cedar complemented with deep green holly leaves. Add a few inches of nandina berries to the vase, and fill with water.

• Create a candle garden centerpiece by grouping assorted pillar candles and votives on a festive plate or platter. Nestle sprigs of greenery, a length of shimmery ribbon, or a bright beaded garland among the candles.

Gifts & Greetings

Instead of the usual card in an envelope and box tied with a bow, you may be sending
all your holiday greetings via E-mail, and your gifts may be homemade videos for family members
living far away. Either way, you'll want to keep a record here for quick reference.

Christmas Card List

NAME	ADDRESS	SENT/RECEIVED

Gift List

NAME	GIFT	SENT/DELIVERED

HANDMADE GREETINGS

•Add a fancy ribbon to dress up purchased cards. Either glue a small bow on the front of the card, or use a paper hole punch and thread ribbon through the holes at the top or around the edges of the card.

•Use seasonal rubber stamps or favorite images cut from old cards, magazines, or wrapping paper to decorate blank purchased cards and envelopes.

FANCY WRAPPING IDEAS

•Glue wrapping paper or adhere contact paper around an empty potato chip can. Fill with cookies, put a bow on top, and tie small candy canes and a gift tag to the bow.

•Glue wide ribbon onto small empty coffee cans. Fill with candies or cookies. Tie a bow around the tin. Add a greenery sprig and a gift tag to the bow.

Holiday Memories

Every holiday season offers its own blend of funny moments, poignant remembrances, and Christmas wishes come true. Be sure you remember every one by writing them on these pages.

TREASURED TRADITIONS

What's the first thing you think of when you think of Christmas? Chances are it's a time-honored family tradition. Write your favorite ones here and maybe include some new ones for next year.

SPECIAL HOLIDAY EVENTS

Whether it's a production of The Nutcracker, *a neighborhood caroling party, or simply a party with close friends, use the space here to write a few of the best memories of these Yuletide happenings.*

HOLIDAY VISITS & VISITORS

There are some friends we seem to see only at Christmas. Take a moment to record all the latest tidbits about growing families and friends' accomplishments that you learn from these annual get-togethers.

Favorite Holiday Recipes

Notes & Ideas for Next Year

THINGS WE LOVED

*List here all the things that worked so well this
Christmas that they must be repeated next year.*

WORKS IN PROGRESS

Here's the place to write ideas for parties, decorations, and recipes that you'd like to try for future holidays.

Party Ideas

Decorations

Recipes

NEW YEAR'S RESOLUTIONS